Celebrating the Centenary of the Great October Revolution

The Russian Revolution and India

Celebrating the Centenary of the Great October Revolution

The Russian Revolution and India

Compilation from *Soviet Land* Magazine and Other Sources

Compiled and Edited by

Ilasai Manian

V. Rajesh

AAKAR

The Russian Revolution and India
Compiled and edited by Ilasai Manian and V. Rajesh

First Published 2019

ISBN 978–93–5002–600–7

Published by
AAKAR BOOKS
28 E Pocket IV, Mayur Vihar Phase I
Delhi 110 091
www.aakarbooks.com

Designed by
Limited Colors, Delhi 110 092

Printed at
Sapra Brothers, Delhi 110 092

Contents

Preface 9

1. India's First Envoys to Revolutionary Russia 13
   Irina Avchina
2. The Story of a Telegram 17
   A.V. Raikov
3. The First Russian Revolution and India 22
   P. Shastitko
4. Tilak and the 1905–1907 Revolution in Russia 27
   A. Raikov
5. Mahatma Gandhi on the Russian Revolution of 1905 32
   Eric Komarov
6. Non-Violence: Gandhi and Lenin 36
   Views of Three Soviet Scholars
7. Tolstoy, Gandhi and India 41
   Chidumbara Raghunathan
8. Galvanising Impact of the October Revolution on India's National-Liberation Movement 47
   G. Adhikari
9. Lenin and the Liberation Struggle in India 52
   E. Komarov
10. India's Response to Lenin 57
    A. Vasilyev

11. Lenin and the Indian Patriots 61
I. Andronov

12. Lenin and Indian Revolutionaries 65
R. Yunitskaya

13. New Light on Bombay Events of 1908 70
A. Vasilyev

14. New Light on Old Indian Revolutionary 74
Ilya Suchkov

15. Progressive Indians and Our Country 83
E. Komarov

16. Pioneers of India's Liberation Movement Acclaimed the October Revolution 93
V.M. Kaul

17. October Revolution and Indian Immigrants in Germany 101
A. Raikov

18. Indian Emigre Revolutionaries in Soviet Russia 106
Alexander Yunel

19. Bhikaji Rustomji Cama and the Russian Revolutionaries 111
P. Shastitko

20. A Russian Revolutionary and His Indian Friends 117
A. Raikov

21. First Mention of Marx in Indian Writings 122
Leonid Mitrokhin

22. Indian Revolutionaries' Pamphlets in Soviet Libraries 126
A. Raikov

23 A Find in the Archives (Documents About an Unknown Indian Mission to Russia in 1859) 129
A. Raikov

24. Visit of Motilal and Jawaharlal Nehru to the USSR in 1927 — 133
A.I. Yunel

25. India's National-Liberation Movement and Socialism at the Start of the 20th Century — 139
A.V. Raikov

26. Recalling the Grim Tragedy of Amritsar — 144
L. Mitrokhin and A. Raikov

27. Lenin and India's Liberation Movement after the October Revolution — 149
E. Komarov

28. Early Contacts Between India and Russia — 152
P.M. Kemp

29. Maxim Gorky and the National Liberation Movement in India — 174
Eve Lyusternik

Preface

This edited book is being released as part of the series on centenary year celebration of the Russian Revolution. It is a compilation of articles on Russian Revolution and Indian national movement published in *Soviet Land, Iscus: Journal of the Indo-Soviet Cultural Society* among other sources. Many of these Soviet era magazines are found scattered in different parts of India. We have found some of these magazines from the collections of Raghunathan Library in Ettayapuram, Tamilnadu. When India attained independence from British colonial rule, the diplomatic ties with the then Soviet Union was established. Embassies of both nations were set up in their respective capitals. The Soviet Information Center of the Soviet embassy in Delhi published *Soviet Land* magazine. The copies of the magazine were sent to different parts of India. The information department of the office of the Soviet embassy in Chennai published *Soviet Nadu* in Tamil language among other press release. In general, the articles that appeared in *Soviet Land* dealt with themes related to the social, economic and cultural development of Soviet Union. Periodically, news related to the inter-governmental cooperation, agreements signed on various issues between Soviet Union and India was analytically reported. To achieve economic self-sufficiency, several agreements were signed by Indian government with Soviet Union to establish heavy industries like iron and steel, oil refinery and so on. Further, inter-governmental cooperation was sought in fostering education and cultural exchange between two countries.

Among others, articles on Indian independence, Russian Revolution appeared in the pages of *Soviet Land* magazine. In particular, the Soviet Indologists wrote articles at regular intervals on Indo-Russian relationship especially the support extended by Russia to the Indian national movement, the relationship between Russian revolutionaries and revolutionary Indian nationalist leaders. At a certain stage in this evolving diplomatic relationship between Soviet Union and India, Soviet Land Nehru Award was instituted. This award was conferred to the writers in India who translated the works of Soviet writers into Indian languages.

For translating Maxim Gorky's *Mother* into Tamil language, the Soviet Land Nehru Award was conferred to T.M.C. Raghunathan (1923-2001). The latter undertook two weeks tour to Soviet Union following the conferment of award. Raghunathan was also conferred Sahitya Akademi Award in Tamil language for his path breaking work on Tamil poet Subramania Bharati titled *Bharati: Kalamum Karuthum*. A versatile literary figure from Tamilnadu, T.M.C. Raghunathan published poetry, short stories, novel, literary criticism, translations, research monographs and journalistic articles. He served as the president of *Tamilnadu Kalai Ilakkiya Perumandram,* the progressive literary-cultural organization associated with the Communist Party of India (CPI) in Tamilnadu. Raghunathan was employed in Soviet Information Centre in Chennai. During this period, he translated the poetry of Soviet writers into Tamil language and published in *Soviet Nadu,* the Tamil edition of *Soviet Land* magazine. His writings on Soviet novelists, short story writers, poets appeared periodically in Press Release. Over a period of time, Raghunathan preserved the copies of *Soviet Nadu* and *Soviet Land* magazines. These volumes were donated to the library established in his memory. While going through the pages of *Soviet Land* magazine, we found several articles and essays concerning the Indian national movement and the support extended by Russia. In particular, the essays related to the lives of the expatriate Indian revolutionaries in Europe and the meeting of Indian revolutionaries with Lenin are of interest in this volume. The views of Indian national leaders like M.K. Gandhi, Jawaharlal Nehru, B.G. Tilak among others on Russian Revolution are also included. In short, this volume will be useful to understand the support extended by Russia to the Indian national movement during the first half of the twentieth century.

Raghunathan Library was established around the personal collection of the writer on themes ranging from poetry, short stories, novel, literary criticism, folklore, history, nationalist movement, philosophy, religious literature to grammar, economics, political science, Marxism and so on. The library houses rare Tamil and English language publications. Raghunathan is a recognized scholar in Tamilnadu on studies related to Subramania Bharati. At a time when he carried out research on Bharati, Raghunathan collected rare books, periodicals, magazines in Tamil language. This included the first editions of poetry, prose and letters of Bharati, books on Bharati by Tamil scholars, newspapers, documents and so on. Based on this extensive collection, Bharati Research Centre was established in Raghunathan library. The library and the research centre has been functioning in Ettayapuram, Tamilnadu in the premises of Bharati Progressive Youth Association, the Ettayapuram youth wing of Tamilnadu Art Literary Federation.

The activities of the Raghunathan Library range from undertaking research on education, art, literature, national movements, social justice, women's studies to aiding research by giving access to the rare collection from the library and research centre. The library also conducts seminars, book release functions periodically. Founded as part of Raghunathan Trust, the library and the research centre is known for its rare collection of books and other resources in Tamilnadu. Doctoral and post-doctoral researchers, masters and undergraduate students have been actively using the library and the research centre over the years. Ilasai Manian, the co-editor of this volume has been the secretary of the trust and personally taking care of the library and the research centre.

We are grateful to A. Sivasubramanian, President of Raghunathan Educational Trust and other members of the trust for their constant encouragement while executing this project. We are also grateful to G. Balamurugan, AIYF Tamilnadu State Secretary for his valuable support during the project. We are thankful to K.K. Saxena of Aakar Books for showing keen interest to publish this volume. We hope the readers will find the articles compiled in this volume useful to understand the relationship between Indian national movement and Russian Revolution.

Ilasai Manian
V. Rajesh

1

India's First Envoys to Revolutionary Russia

Irina Avchina

The October Revolution paved the way for real prospects for the national liberation movement in the colonial and dependent countries of the East. The first actions of the Soviet Government, the Decree on Peace, the Appeal to All Working Moslems of Russia and the East, the Declaration on the Rights of the Peoples of Russia, which proclaimed the basic principles of the new state's national policy, received a wide response in the colonial countries. All the fighters for national independence ardently hailed the policy of the Soviet Republic.

Social and political organisations of many colonial and dependent countries desired to establish contact with Soviet Russia. From the end of 1918 Moscow played host to delegations of the revolutionary organisations of almost all countries of the East. The envoys of India also visited the capital of the new-born Soviet republic.

Recently in its archives has been discovered a document dealing with the sojourn of India's first delegation in the Soviet capital.

The envoys of India reached Moscow in November 1918. In an attempt to throw the British intelligence service off the tracks, they used false names. They called themselves Muhammed Hadi and Ahmat Haris.

The Indian guests handed over to the People's Commissar of Foreign Affairs in Moscow a message from the people of India. It hailed the lofty principles of the Soviet policy and appealed for support to the Indian people striving for independence.

Meeting with Lenin

On 23 November, 1918, the Indian delegation was received by V.I. Lenin in the Kremlin. A lengthy conversation took place. The proclamation issued soon afterwards stated: "In mid-November 1918 two representatives of Indian Moslems, of the inhabitants of the city of Delhi and the learned professions... arrived here and introduced themselves to our leader Lenin. They explained to him a great deal concerning India and the East."

On 25 November the Indian guests attended the session of the All-Russian Central Executive Committee.

"Comrades and brothers, leaders of the Russian Revolution," states one of the Indian delegates in his address of greetings, "India greets you from afar for the victory you have scored in the cause of world progress... India bows before the noble mission that fell to Russia. India prays and begs to providence that it should send you the strength to complete the work you've begun and that your ideas should spread all over the earth." (From verbatim report of the session of the All-Russian Central Executive Committee, Central State Archives of the October Revolution.)

"We may derive confidence from the greetings we have just heard," stated Y.M. Sverdlov, Head of the Soviet state, "that all the oppressed cast their eyes towards Soviet Russia... . If the revolution has been echoed in far-off India then... not far off is the time when the enslaved peoples of Asia will finally free themselves... . Permit me to send greetings... to the people of India." (*Modern and Current History,* 1957 p. 121.)

Special Memorandum

The same day the Indian guests presented to Y.M. Sverdlov a special memorandum which was published in the Soviet newspapers under the headline "The Voice of Enslaved India".

"Leaders of the Russian Revolution, Comrades, Friends! Permit us to thank you for the happiness of talking with you personally and transmit to you the greetings on behalf of the Indian people and 70 million Indian Moslems. Permit us to convey greetings to the Russian Revolution, which has instilled new hope in us and showed us the new path of struggle."

"The world does not know," the memorandum stated, "what is taking place in India". There followed the mournful story of the sufferings of the people of India.

The memorandum pointed out that the representatives of India who had wished to present their demands were prohibited from entering England; that the Indian representatives were put in prison both in the United States and France, and that they were expelled from Japan, Switzerland and Denmark under the pressure of British diplomats.

"The revolution in Russia," it went on further, "created a tremendous impression on the psychology of the Indian people. Despite all the efforts of England, the slogan of self-determination of nations has penetrated into India."

The memorandum wound up with the following words: "We hope that our brothers from the great, free Russia will stretch out a hand to us in the cause of the liberation of India and the whole world. We are convinced that all the freedom-loving people will see the day when 325 million Indians... will be freed from the bondage and slavery of foreign authorities." (*Izvestia*, 26 November, 1918).

In accepting the memorandum, Y.M. Sverdlov said: "I have listened to all that has been said with great satisfaction... . We authorise the Indian representatives to convey the best wishes of the Executive Committee and our hopes for the earliest liberation of the Indian people."

To this very day it is unknown who the first envoys of the Indian people were. Their real names are not known. And only 40 years later documents were found in Moscow in the archives of Kolchak's counter-revolutionary Siberian government from which it followed that the British intelligence service did, after all, manage to get on their tracks. What happened to them? This question is still awaiting an answer.

(Press Release: Issued by the Information Department,
USSR Embassy in India, October 1967)

2

The Story of a Telegram

A.V. Raikov

In October 1917, on the eve of the Great October Socialist Revolution, a telegram was received by the Petrograd Soviet of Workers' and Soldiers' Deputies from Indian democrats resident in Stockholm. It read as follows (text retranslated from Russian):

"Revolutionary Russia is striving to achieve a lasting peace on the basis of the principle of self-determination of people. The instructions to Mr. Skobelev, who is being sent to Paris, do not correspond to these aims, as the basic problems of India, Egypt and Ireland have been left out. The Indians, the Egyptians and the Irish are conscious of their natural right to complete self-determination. The liberation movement of these people has acquired such a scale that no stable peace is possible without a positive solution of their problems. In the name of fidelity to the ideals of the Russian Revolution and because of the great importance of the liberation of India for Russia and the whole world, we urge the Workers' and Soldiers' Soviet to continue fearlessly and unyieldingly fighting against the ruthless British imperialism both at the Paris conference and during peace negotiations."

This telegram, published in the newspaper *Novaya Zhizn*, aroused a good deal of interest in the Russian press at that time.

But how had the Indian patriots found themselves in Stockholm? Why did they turn for assistance to the Petrograd Soviet and with what results?

Facts relating to this episode have only recently been brought to light through the efforts of Indologists in the USSR and the German Democratic Republic.

The presence of a group of Indian revolutionaries in Stockholm in 1917 was connected with the activities of the Berlin Committee of Indian Nationalists formed in Germany during World War I. At that time a number of Indian patriots had entertained the idea of liberating their country from the British rule with the help of Germany which was England's enemy in the war. A group of prominent Indian revolutionaries had been active in Berlin. However, soon the Indian patriots became disillusioned about their "allies". They realised that Germany's aims in the war had little to do with the liberation of India. Virendra Chattopadhaya, well-known Indian revolutionary, wrote in one of his letters in 1918: "We are regarded as pawns in the German game to be used only when they need us."

As a result and also on account of worsening relations with the German ruling circles, the Indian revolutionaries decided to build their own centre in a neutral country and chose Stockholm for this purpose. In May 1917, the Berlin Committee deputed Chattopadhaya there; he was soon followed by M.P.T. Acharya and other revolutionaries. Thus the Stockholm Bureau of the Berlin Committee of Indian Nationalists came into existence. The creation of this Bureau was a very timely step which proved more effective than had been expected.

A large number of European social-democrats had gathered at Stockholm at the time, and the Indian revolutionaries looked towards them for help. They contacted prominent figures of the Second International regarding them as representatives of the European workers' movement. But here also disillusionment awaited them. Virendra Chattopadhaya and the other Indian patriots soon saw for themselves that the Right-wing social-democrats did not show any interest in the struggle of the Indian people for independence. In another letter Chattopadhaya wrote bitterly: "We all have the feeling that the question of subject nations is being deliberately ignored or put off by the socialists." Under these conditions, it was quite natural that the Indian patriots should turn their close attention to that international power which was consistently and resolutely raising the question of self-determination of nations and elimination of colonial oppression. This power was represented by the Russian Bolsheviks.

When Chattopadhaya arrived in Stockholm, the February Revolution had already taken place in Russia. Autocracy had been overthrown and a provisional bourgeois government had assumed office. The Bolshevik Party was preparing for a proletarian revolution. Party centres were active outside Russia also. In Stockholm there was a representation of the Central Committee of the RSDLP (B) which issued a Bulletin of the Russian Revolution published in German, as also another periodical—*"Pravda's" Russian Correspondent*. They carried material concerning the revolutionary events in Russia, the strategy and tactics of the Bolsheviks and articles by V.I. Lenin. The Indian revolutionaries were acquainted with these papers and consequently with Lenin's name. There are documents in archives in India which confirm this. Thus, for instance, the British Ambassador in Sweden, reporting on the arrival of Chattopadhaya in Stockholm, expressed his belief that his "intention was to get Lenin or other anti-British Russian extremists to work for the Indian independence movement in Russia".

The ambassador was not far from the truth at least in one respect: Chattopadhaya was indeed anxious to meet Lenin. Speaking in 1934 at a conference of the Leningrad branch of the USSR Academy of Sciences he said that when early in May 1917 he had arrived in Stockholm he had found many emigres there from different countries and had asked whether Lenin was also among them. He had been greatly disappointed that he was not able to meet him.

The Indian patriots working in Europe no doubt knew of the Bolsheviks' standpoint on major international problems, of their views on the national problem and of their principled opposition to the policy of the imperialists. Therefore, very soon they established direct contact with the Russian Bolsheviks in Stockholm, as they saw in them their true allies in the struggle for freedom. At the same time they carefully watched the position taken by the Provisional Government on the colonial question. A conference of the allied states of the *Entente* was to take place in Paris in 1917 at which the aims of the war under the new conditions were to be discussed. It became known to the Indian revolutionaries that the instructions given to Skobelev, the representative of the bourgeois Provisional Government in Russia, did not include the question of India's independence. That is why they turned for help not to the Provisional Government, but to the Petrograd Soviet, conscious as they must have been that in the Bolshevik faction they would find support. And they were satisfied that their telegram elicited a positive response from the Bolsheviks who utilised it in their struggle against the opportunist and reactionary parties. The telegram also received publicity abroad, as it was published in the German press.

The Indian patriots were most keen to establish closer relations with revolutionary Russia, and on 1 November 1917, Chattopadhaya sent to Berlin a plan for the development of cooperation with revolutionary Russia which he drew up with the help of Troyanovsky, a Russian Bolshevik. Their contacts were so close that Chattopadhaya appended to the plan a memorandum entitled "Project of Russian-Indian Rapprochement" which contained some important ideas on the necessity of mutual action on the part of revolutionary people of Russia and the oppressed people of the East. Troyanovsky, on his part, laid special stress on the importance of an organised mass movement.

The contacts of the Indian emigres with the Bolsheviks became particularly strong after the victory of the Socialist Revolution in Russia, when they saw for themselves that the first socialist state in the world was a true ally in their struggle. The activity of the Stockholm centre increased after the October Revolution. The Indians helped to publish various information material in the Russian language. It was only natural, therefore, that the question of a representative of the Stockholm Bureau going to Petrograd should have come up.

Troyanovsky invited Chattopadhaya to visit the city, and he readily accepted the invitation as he had long wished to meet Lenin and see for himself the revolutionary changes which had taken place in Russia. However, the German government was decidedly against it. An official German report of that period stated that Chattopadhaya had completely identified himself with the Bolsheviks. Very indignant, Chattopadhaya wrote:

"It is true that Troyanovsky is an opponent of German imperialism, as well as of every other imperialism. But there is really no reason why he cannot work for the Indian cause and in this way against England. Are we ourselves not against every form of imperialism?"

When Troyanovsky returned to Russia, the People's Commissariat of Foreign Affairs with his assistance sent through the Soviet diplomatic representative in Stockholm another invitation to Chattopadhaya to visit Russia, but the latter could not avail of it either. It was only after the defeat of Germany that Chattopadhaya and his comrades from the Stockholm Bureau and the Berlin Committee at last managed to visit Soviet Russia.

The above facts add considerably to our knowledge of early contacts between Indians and the Russian Bolsheviks. It would now seem that the first to establish friendly relations with the Bolsheviks were the Indian patriots in Stockholm.

(*Soviet Land*, October 1967)

3

The First Russian Revolution and India

P. Shastitko

The Russian Revolution of 1905 was the first revolution of the epoch of imperialism and the first also of the 20th century. It gave a mighty impetus to mankind's revolutionary development and became a new milestone in its history. The period of short-term relative social peace was over. Capitalism entered, a phase of severe crises.

The peculiarity of the Russian revolution was that it set before itself bourgeois-democratic tasks. The proletariat assumed the leadership of the struggle and drew into that struggle broad lower strata of society. "The peculiarity of the Russian revolution", said V.I. Lenin, "is that it was a bourgeois-democratic revolution in its social content, but a proletarian revolution in its methods of struggle." The revolution started in Petersburg and Moscow, where the streets were blocked by barricades set up by the fighting workers. Then it spread to other industrial centres of Russia, where mass-scale strikes broke out. The sweep and tempo of the struggle increased. The poor peasants were drawn into its vortex and they started destroying the landlords' estates; the revolution spread to the outlying regions of Russia inhabited by oppressed nationalities: Poland, Finland (then parts of the Russian Empire), Transcaucasia and Central Asia. Importantly, the advanced ranks of the proletariat, the poorest sections of the peasantry and the nationalities oppressed by tsarism unitedly fought the common enemy-tsarist autocracy. What was at stake was not only the right of nation to self-determination, but also the international class interests of the proletariat and the working people generally. In a number of cities, even certain units of the Army—the sole support of the odious tsarist regime—backed the masses. Sadly, the bulk of the Army remained loyal to the autocratic regime during the first Russian revolution.

Despite the heroism and self-sacrifice of the revolutionary masses, the first attempt to overthrow the tsarist autocracy was unsuccessful: reaction proved to be stronger. But, despite the failure, the first Russian revolution greatly influenced the international working-class movement. The Russian proletariat deservedly came to be regarded as one of the most militant and organised sections of the world revolutionary front. The new organisational forms—the Soviets, spontaneously set up by the masses in the course of their struggle—and the militant methods tested in practice—armed rebellion and general strike—were rightly included in the arsenal of weapons of the world revolutionary movement. "The proletariat of the whole world is now looking eagerly towards the proletariat of Russia," said Lenin. "The overthrow of tsarism in Russia, so valiantly begun by our working class, will be the turning point in the history of all countries, it will facilitate the task of the workers of all nations, in all states, in all parts of the globe."

The Russian revolution was enthusiastically welcomed in the East. It gave a boost to the national-liberation struggle of the colonial and dependent countries, the ground for which had already been prepared by the course of internal development: the rapacious exploitation of these countries and the destruction of their traditional socio-economic structure. But there was no "export of revolution". That was a pure fabrication of reactionary propaganda. The development of capitalism and the emergence on the political scene of new classes—the proletariat and the bourgeoisie—and their parties created the conditions for future social upheavals. The Russian revolution speeded up these developments: in 1905–1911 a revolution broke out in Iran, in 1908–1909, in Turkey, and in 1911–1913, in China. The national-liberation movement in other countries of the East also gained in tempo.

The long-suffering, oppressed people of India soon learnt about the Russian revolution. The Indian public watched with interest and sympathy the fierce social battles being waged in the North. At the Calcutta session of the Indian National Congress in 1906, the President of the Congress, Dadabhai Naoroji, declared: "If Russian peasants are not only prepared for self-government, but have also managed to snatch it from the hands of the world's greatest autocracy, if China in the east of Asia and Persia in the west are awaking, if Japan has already awoken, if Russia is heroically fighting for its liberation, how can we, allegedly free citizens of the Indo-British Empire, remain subjects of despotism deprived of all rights?" At the Calcutta session, the demand for *swaraj* was put forward for the first time. The experience of the Russian revolution had induced the Indian public to raise radical demands.

The Russian revolution helped draw into the national-liberation struggle new social forces in Asian countries and called on them to play a prominent part in history. Thus, in India the working class, which appeared on the political scene for the first time, borrowed from its Russian brothers the weapon of strike, which had been so effectively used in the first Russian revolution, and introduced it in Indian practice. The days of petitioning, of the collection of signatures, were at last over. Now the Indians learnt how effective the methods of the proletariat's political struggle were. In 1907, the railwaymen of the Punjab went on a strike. Mass protests were launched in industrial Calcutta. The clerks of the East Indian Railway declared a strike. The year 1908 saw the well-known strike of Bombay workers in protest against the arrest by British authorities of the leader of India's freedom-struggle, B.G. Tilak. Commenting on this strike, V.I. Lenin wrote: "In India, too, the proletariat has already developed to conscious political mass struggle—and, that being the case, the Russian-style British regime in India is doomed!"

B.G. Tilak displayed keen interest in the Russian revolution. In one of his articles, he wrote: "When in Russia representatives of both lower and upper classes—professors and students, workers and factory workers, editors and shop-owners—organised strikes everywhere and, being afraid of nothing, boldly and persistently presented their demands to the tsar, the mightiest of all monarchs, who had a more than two-million-strong army, the tsar of all Russia had to meet his subjects' demands." Russia's example inspired the Indians to wage a resolute struggle and instilled in them confidence in their victory. Even those who had at first hesitated and feared Britain's might were inspired by this example and drawn into the struggle. Thousands upon thousands of Indian patriots were moved by a sense of hurt national pride and a desire to uphold the honour of their motherland. Quite typical in this respect was a leaflet distributed in Bengal: "Bengalis! Do not despair because of lack of arms! Look at Russia! See the way they are accomplishing a revolution. You must do the same. The most important thing is courage. Be courageous and do not regret the lack of arms. Look around and you will find arms."

Indian national revolutionaries, both in India and abroad, carefully studied the experience of the Russian revolution. Indian revolutionary groups were formed in London and then in Paris. They established close contacts with Russian Social-Democrats. For instance, the well-known Indian revolutionary Krishnavarma and Madame Cama had a meeting with the prominent Russian Social-Democrat and Orientalist M. Pavlovich. Later, Pavlovich recalled: "Cama showed great interest in the Russian revolutionary development, especially the 1905 revolution, the role of the working class in the movement and read something on Marxist theory." Cama took part in the International Socialist Congress in Stuttgart and delivered at the congress a passionate speech full of revolutionary enthusiasm. She said: "Our people cannot send their delegates, since they are too poor, but I believe that the day of their awakening will come, and they will follow the Russian comrades, to whom we sent our fraternal greetings."

Cama submitted a draft resolution demanding the complete abolition of British colonial rule in India.

The Indian patriots drew for themselves another important conclusion from the experience of the Russian revolution: in order to defeat a strong, experienced and well-organised enemy, it is necessary to win over the army to their side. The newspaper of the Bengali revolutionaries, *Jugantar*, declared in August 1907: "The Russian revolution has shown that even in the tsarist troops there are many adherents to the revolution. The same was the case during the French revolution. The revolutionaries have, extra opportunities where state power is in the hands of foreigners, since the latter draft soldiers mainly from among their subjects... When the time of collision with the government comes, the revolutionaries will win these troops over to their side and obtain the arms they received from the authorities."

Needless to say, at that time, the Russian revolution influenced comparatively small sections of the Indian people. The establishment of the first ties between the advanced circles of the Indian national-liberation movement and the international socialist movement did not as yet mean the broad popularisation of the ideas of scientific socialism in India. But the glow which shone over the Himalayas was seen by the Indian people, long suffering under the colonial yoke, and kindled in their hearts the hope for freedom.

(*Soviet Land*, Feburary 1977)

4

Tilak and the 1905–1907 Revolution in Russia

A. Raikov

At the end of the last, and the beginning of our century when the Indian liberation movement was in the formative stage there was strong desire among the Indian patriots to make use of the experience of the Russian revolutionaries. At the turn of the century, Indian patriots changed their opinion about Russia. Earlier they had associated the government with the people in Russia. Following the First Russian Revolution of 1905–1907, a tendency to dissociate the Russian people from the government and to express sympathies with the revolutionary movement in Russia developed among Indian patriots. The more prominent a leader in the Indian liberation movement, the quicker and a more distinct change came about in his views.

This could well be seen from the activities and views of Bal Gangadhar Tilak (1856–1920), that outstanding leader of the liberation movement, who spearheaded the Left Wing in the Indian National Congress.

People are very well aware of Tilak's reaction to the anti-Russian campaign in the British colonial press. It shouted about a "Russian threat" to the Indians and systematically "exposed" the despotism of the Russian autocracy. In his interview to the British correspondent Nevinson, Tilak noted: "I know the worst that you can say about the Russian bureaucracy but even that bureaucracy does according to its lights seek to maintain the honour and prosperity of Russia because Russia is its own country. Our bureaucracy administers a country not its own, but for the sake of a country far away, entirely different in character and interests. Our bureaucracy is despotic, alien and absentee".

Such was Tilak's response to the campaign of Russophobia. Moreover, he was ready to use Russia's assistance in the struggle for the freedom of his country. Tilak, thus, acted in keeping with the age-old tradition of the Indian people who had long ago connected their hopes of liberation with Russia. This is evident from Russian archival documents, some of which were discovered only recently.

Of great interest is the fact that on his own initiative Tilak contacted the Russian Consul in Bombay. He met him on more than one occasion, trying with his assistance, to solve problems pertaining to the main goal of his life, which he formulated as follows: "Swaraj is my birthright and I will have it". As time passed Tilak's views on the ways to attain Indian independence changed.

At the beginning of 1905 he apparently considered quite possible for the Indians to change over to violent methods in their struggle, including an armed uprising, and began preparing for it in his own way. He believed that it would be necessary to have Indian officers with up-to-date military education. Since the colonisers had hindered Indians from acquiring that education, Tilak and his supporters resolved to send patriotic young people to study in other countries.

Counting on assistance from Russia in that undertaking, Tilak entered into negotiations with Russian Consul V.O. Klemm. Tilak preferred the Consulate of Russia, in spite of the fact that those of Germany, the Austro-Hungarian Monarchy, and other countries were also there in Bombay at that time.

On 9 January, 1905, that is, before the Russian Revolution, Tilak for the first time made a request to Klemm for helping Indians enter one of Russia's military colleges. The next day the Russian Counsul sent a message to St. Petersburg about Tilak's visit. That message is of major interest, because it sheds light both on Tilak's views and the goals of Russian diplomats in India.

The Congress "extremist" leader explained his turning to Russia by the following circumstances: Indians believed in the might of Russia, in spite of its failures in the Japanese war, and they were attracted by Russian affability and sympathy with Eastern nations, which was hardly to be expected from any other European country.

The reasons which Tilak mentioned for his visit reflected the feelings prevalent among rather broad sections of Indians towards Russia. Tilak wanted to learn from the Russian Consul whether Indians could be admitted to Russian military schools. He said: "We would like to send several young men of good lineage to get a military education in some country and Russia seems the most suitable to us", (translated from Russian—Ed.). Tilak frankly explained the purpose as follows: "We need people whose knowledge would be truly as good as, or, if possible, better than that of the British officers, in all arms of the service, not only in infantry and artillery" (translated from Russian—Ed.).

Klemm was considerate towards Tilak's request. However, the Russian Tsarist Government was apparently against any actions that could cause discontent among the British, shrunk away from its fulfilment. On March 18, 1905, Consul Klemm reported to St. Petersburg: "Brahmin Gangadhar Tilak called on me for an answer. I told him that, according to the information which I had received from St. Petersburg, foreign subjects are admitted to our military training establishments in no other way but with the permission of their governments". On his own initiative Consul Klemm advised Tilak to send young people to French schools so that "at the first opportunity for them they could go to Russia". Tilak answered that he would discuss the suggestion with his friends.

It is significant that in the course of talks with the Russian Consul, Tilak's position gradually changed. The Russian revolution exerted a tremendous influence on the political situation in the Eastern countries, including India. One can see from Klemm's reports that Tilak very quickly responded to the changed situation in Russia. After a regular meeting with Tilak, the Russian consul reported: "Tilak said his friends and he had already come to the conclusion that at present it would be, perhaps, not quite convenient to send young people to Russia". The reason for those changed plans had been exactly in the revolution. "He hinted", Consul Klemm went on, "at the internal complications in Russia, which the local press tries its best to picture as a full-fledged revolution".

While attentively studying Tilak's statements about the Russian revolution in subsequent years, one can see entirely new tendencies in his approach to the methods of struggle for independence. Under the influence of the developments taking place in Russia he became much more interested than before in various aspects of the mass movement. If one comprehensively studies the question of training Indian regular officers, one can come to a conclusion that Tilak gradually lost interest in that. For instance, he declined to send Indian boys to a military college, although the Russian Government had given its consent.

It seems that contacts with the Russian consul were maintained only mechanically. For instance, instead of a group of Indians, only one, Captain Madhavrao Jadhav, was sent to Europe. Klemm reported: "At Tilak's request, I took the liberty of giving him a letter of recommendation to our Consul-General". It should be noted, that the consul showed such goodwill and sincere desire for helping that young man which had been hardly stipulated in the instructions given to him. When, with the support of Russian diplomats, Madhavrao Jadhav was invited to military classes in Switzerland, he was financed through Klemm, at Tilak's request.

The opinion of Zhadovsky, Russian envoy in Switzerland, about Captain Madhavrao Jadhav is very interesting. Having met that Indian, Zhadovsky reported to St. Petersburg: "After my conversation with him, I have certain doubts about the fact that military classes are a true or the only reason for his coming to Europe.... According to the nature of the questions of interest to him, pertaining to anything but military operations, but rather revolving round a dream about liberating his country from the foreign rule in other ways, he looks like a politician, maybe a sincere patriot, but certainly by no means a military man. "His intentions are mysterious to me."

On the basis of Zhadovsky's report a conclusion can be drawn that Madhavrao was more probably fulfilling other assignments for Tilak. For instance, he was trying to establish contacts with the patriotic organisations of Indian emigrants in other countries, or with the appropriate sections of the European public.

After the signing of the British-Russian agreement, in 1907, Russian diplomats stopped contacts with Madhavrao. There was no point in the meetings between the Russian Consul and Tilak. In his articles and public speeches, Tilak popularised the ways of struggle used by Russian revolutionaries and called upon Indians to follow their example.

The contacts between Tilak and Klemm, discussed in this article, reflected a stage in Tilak's evolution. There was a period when Tilak hoped to use imperialist contradictions for the purpose of the liberation movement. After 1907 everything fell into place. While popularising the experience of the Russian revolution, Tilak could not have anything in common with diplomats from Tsarist Russia. So, he broke contacts with them.

(*Soviet Land,* March 1967)

5

Mahatma Gandhi on the Russian Revolution of 1905

Eric Komarov

We all know what an important ideological influence was exercised by the great Russian writer Leo Tolstoy on Mahatma Gandhi's world outlook. It was by no means fortuitous that Gandhi called Tolstoy his "teacher". It would be wrong, however, to assume that Gandhi's interest in Russia was confined to Leo Tolstoy. The latter's influence was in itself, occasioned by the historic role which Russia began to play in the world at the turn of the century. History had made Russia the centre of an imminent transformation of the world at the very time that Gandhi was acquainting himself with the teachings of Tolstoy, whose works had acquired international fame. This was soon confirmed by the first Russian revolution of 1905 which was the prologue to the triumph of the Great October Socialist Revolution of 1917. However, while still at the threshold of the 20th century, Russia with its active ideological life and strike struggles attracted the attention of progressive people and had a growing influence on the liberation movement in different countries. The lively interest shown by Mahatma Gandhi and other progressive Indians in Russia was an extremely important evidence of this historical process. For instance, already in the '90s of the last century Swami Vivekananda spoke of Russia's leading role in the coming re-making of the world.

Mahatma Gandhi's interest in Russia was awakened by the works of Leo Tolstoy who, as V.I. Lenin pointed out, reflected the smouldering resentment against the existing system, the "maturing aspiration for improvement". And when the revolutionary events of 1905 took place in Russia, Mahatma Gandhi—who was at that time fighting racial oppression in South Africa—immediately responded enthusiastically. In 1905, Gandhi repeatedly wrote about the Russian events in his paper *Indian Opinion*, regarding them as an inspiring and instructive example of the liberation struggle. At that time also, he published short feature stories about prominent historical figures of different countries and epochs, who had fought selflessly against oppression and defended lofty human values. These two types of publications in the *Indian Opinion*—reports of the revolutionary events in Russia and sketches of eminent champions of truth—served one and the same aim: to imbue people with freedom-loving aspirations, with humanism. They merged, as it were, in two feature stories carried by the paper, one of which was devoted to Leo Tolstoy, and the other to Maxim Gorky. Further, when writing about Gorky, Gandhi openly and directly spoke about the liberation struggle in Russia. For Gorky was one of the most active participants in the Russian revolution, its "Stormy Petrel". Mahatma Gandhi was probably the first Indian to write specifically about Gorky. And although the information at his disposal in South Africa, so far away from Russia, was scanty, the very fact that he addressed himself to Gorky was proof of the great Indian's broad world outlook and showed how far the fame of the "Stormy Petrel" of the Russian revolution had spread.

In an essay published in Gujarati in the *Indian Opinion* on 1 July 1905, Mahatma Gandhi spoke of the resemblance "up to a point" between Russia and India. He cited two facts: the poverty of the people and the autocratic, oppressive rule in both the countries—the power of the Tsar in Russia and of the "British Raj" in India. Incidentally, this resemblance was also noted by V. I. Lenin who spoke of the "hunger strikes" in Russia and India and of the "Russian-style British regime in India".

Gandhi drew this comparison between Russia and India for a very definite purpose: to show his countrymen that oppression could and should be fought and that was what the Russians were doing. He completed his comparison of the two countries with the following words: "Seeing such oppression, some Russians do come out bravely against it from time to time;" It is not surprising, therefore, that in Gorky Gandhi saw, first and foremost, a bold fighter against the Tsariat autocracy—"one of the chief participants in the rebellion in Russia" and a champion of the people. And this, wrote Gandhi, was not an accidental fact because Gorky himself came from the people, had been "brought up in extreme poverty, educating himself through his own efforts". Further, he describes Gorky's socio-political position: "He wrote many things, all of them with a single purpose, viz., to stir up the people against the tyrannies they were labouring under, to warn the authorities and to render public services, in so far as this was possible. Without caring to make money, he writes with such vehemence and bitterness that the authorities keep a stern eye on him. He has also been to jail in the service of the people and considers imprisonment an honour. It is said that there is no other writer in Europe who is as great a champion of people's rights as Maxim Gorky."

In Gorky, Gandhi did not see (and, indeed, he could not have seen in the circumstances in which he was waging his struggle) a writer standing for the ideological positions of the labour movement, of socialism. He interpreted Gorky's activities in accordance with his own ideas of how the struggle against political oppression should be waged. Hence, for instance, his reference to "warning the authorities", whereas the fact is that Gorky did not strive to warn the authorities or make them listen to reason, but sought to bring about their overthrow by revolutionary means. Nevertheless, in spite of certain elements of a liberal-reformist approach, Mahatma Gandhi laid the main stress on resistance to oppression. Gorky impressed him precisely on this count. The developing liberation struggle in Russia inspired him precisely because it was an example of such resistance. And in 1906, he wrote—this was obviously a fling at the Indian liberals, the Moderates—that in Russia the people "were not limiting themselves to petitions", but were acting.

Gandhi told his readers about the country-wide political strike in Russia in October 1905, which delighted him as an example of organised mass action. Gandhi said this "was a great lesson to us" and wrote: "We, too, can resort to the Russian remedy against tyranny." Already at that time, in his own way, he foresaw, he sensed the historical significance of the maturing Russian Revolution. He wrote: "If the Russian people succeed, this revolution in Russia will be regarded as the greatest victory, the greatest event of the present century."

In his article, Mahatma Gandhi paid tribute not only to the "Stormy Petrel" of the Russian Revolution but to the revolution of 1905 itself, which he hailed and the experience of which he sought to make use of. At that time Gorky, well aware of India's incipient awakening to the struggle for freedom, profoundly sympathised with this struggle and strove to acquaint the Russian progressive public with it more widely. Writing to the Indian patriot Shyamaji Krishnavarma in 1912, Maxim Gorky described the Indians as a people who had given to mankind the most profound insight into the human intellect, and said: "We must make known one people to the other, so that everybody who thirsts for justice, who desires to live in harmony with reason, should understand their unity, the unity of their aims, their spirit, and should be united in one invincible force, which will conquer finally all the evil in the world."

(*Soviet Land*, October 1972)

6

Non-Violence: Gandhi and Lenin

Views of Three Soviet Scholars

The Soviet Review Discussion Club recently discussed the subject of non-violence as a human value, in which some very leading Soviet Indologists participated. Almost all of them agreed in the end that there should be a critical attitude to everything including Gandhism, Marxism, violence and non-violence. Given below are the views in brief of the three of those Indologists. —Editor

Dr O. Martyshin D.Sc. (Law)

Marx attached no absolute importance either to violence or to non-violence. So it appears to be a question of balance, of the right combination of different means to achieve one's end. That applies to both international and national aspects mentioned by Dr Kutsenkov and Dr. Chicherov, who seem to urge a reappraisal of exactly this issue.

The world is saturated with violence, it is on the brink of disaster. The issue of survival leads us to determine our attitude towards violence—both in regard to regional conflicts and to national liberation struggles. There is an urgent need to make the utmost of alternative methods—peaceful, non-violent or whatever you choose to call them. We all have to stop and consider whether our habit of resorting to force might not lead to global conflict. One major concern of the Soviet Union, the USA and other nations today is how to ensure that local conflicts do not escalate into global confrontations. Yet no country and no people can now afford to ignore the global survival issue, which is the concern of all.

I think Dr. Kutsenkov asserted that being a co-author of the Delhi Declaration does not mean adopting the philosophy of Mahatma Gandhi. But once he starts contrasting ethics with reason—ethics in Gandhi and Tolstoy, and reason in the Delhi Declaration—I cannot agree with him.

That may apply to Tolstoy. But he was not a politician. Gandhi, however, attached great importance to reason—because he was a politician. As a great politician he was an apostle of non-violence. If Gandhi had not been a politician, I don't believe he would have been so famous as an advocate of non-violence and received global recognition. The paramount concern today is survival. Everyone wants to live. And exactly this desire puts the concept of non-violence in international affairs on a new foundation, and calls for a new attitude towards it.

Finally, morality is of exceptional importance both in international relations and in the upholding of principles for a non-violent world. The modern world badly needs such personalities as Tolstoy and Gandhi.

Dr A. Litman D.Sc. (History)

The imperative need for a new way of political thinking raises the question of the purpose and meaning of common human values in our time. The question of human values per se has not yet received proper treatment in our social science. The call to step up research into new social phenomena and processes is directed at Indologists and all those who are concerned with Indian culture and with the human values it contains.

Our works on Mahatma Gandhi and his teaching have concentrated on the class nature of the principle of non-violence, and in effect, have ignored its humanistic substance.

Lenin stressed that Marxist theory had never made violence the sole and indispensable condition for worker's emancipation. Lenin said: "To talk about 'violence' in general, without examining the conditions which distinguish reactionary from revolutionary violence, means being a Philistine who renounces revolution, or else it means simply deceiving oneself and others by sophistry."

At this point, it would be worth noting that under Lenin's leadership, the fledgeling Soviet Republic developed its relations with other nations, particularly with the countries of the Orient, on the basis of non-violence. "The Soviet Republic enjoys tremendous popularity among all the Eastern people (...) because they see in us an unswerving fighter against imperialism, because ours is the only Republic (...) which is capable of utilising every situation without the use of force, and which is also able to gain a victory by renouncing the use of force."

The realities of our world, primarily the threat of nuclear disaster as well as a growing awareness of the inter-relationship, inter-dependence, integrity, and unity of mankind, all underline the need for a new philosophy to cover the sphere of human values too, and non-violence, in particular.

Admittedly, it was Mahatma Gandhi who made the most detailed and comprehensive interpretation of the principle of non-violence.

I will talk about the general feature of the Gandhian concept as a human value. The starting point here is that non-violence is a principle inherent in human nature rather than enforced from without. Urging popular non-violent action against British rule, Gandhi specified ways of applying this universal human principle.

It is important to understand that Gandhi asserted that non-violence differed from inaction. (And on this point, I do not agree with Dr Kutsenkov). From the very start of his activities in South Africa to his death, he firmly held the view that there had to be a definite borderline between non-violent struggle and passive non-resistance. Pointing to the adverse practical effects of combining non-violence and inaction, he constantly emphasised the active, creative and constructive character of non-violence. He urged India to adhere to this principle not out of weakness but because it ought to be aware of its own strength and power.

Indicatively, even at the dawn of the nuclear age, Gandhi saw the dangers inherent in nuclear weapons. Less than a year before his tragic death, he wrote that the West longed for wisdom; that it despaired as the stocks of atomic weapons grew, because they meant the total destruction of the West, and indeed of the entire world. In the face of a possible nuclear holocaust, Gandhi grew even more convinced that non-violence alone was the inevitable and most effective means of settling all international disputes. Only non-violence could save the human race. Gandhi expected India to play a leading part in promoting the principle of non-violence in international relations, and he was certain that India was destined to help turn non-violence as a human value into the underlying principle of peaceful human existence.

The events of the past few years, and, indeed, the Indian foreign policy as a whole have to a certain extent, borne out these predictions and hopes of Gandhi. It is safe to say that the Delhi Declaration embodies Gandhi's ideas of non-violence as a human value.

There is a well-known tenet that the human race sets itself only such objectives as it can achieve; therefore, these objectives result from historical development itself. It is no accident that the architects of the Delhi Declaration are two great nations with different socio-political systems.

This alone is evidence that social development itself has now made it imperative for nations to translate the ideal of non-violence as a human value into practice. The Delhi Declaration came as an expression of this urgent need and as a triumph of political realism and high humanism. It states, in part, that peaceful coexistence must become the universal norm of international relations, and that non-violence must be the basis of human society.

Dr. A. Chicherov D.Sc. (History)

Dr. Litman is right when he says that we have underestimated non-violence as a principle of political struggle.

However, when he argues that any kind of violence is a bad thing, I think he swings to the other extreme. Even Mahatma Gandhi did not reject all kinds of violence. You may recall differences of opinion within the Indian national liberation movement, and that Nehru was even critical of Mahatma Gandhi making a fetish of non-violence.

I would like to emphasise that when we speak of non-violence as a human principle, what we have in mind is, rejection of physical violence. There is likely to be widespread consensus on this fact.

But if we reject all forms of violence, political included, I would urge further consideration of the issue. The Decree on Peace—that's fine, of course. Yet, was the Decree on Power and the Decree on Land violence? I invite you consider it carefully that popular non-violent movement meant violence in regard to those in power. Yet it was violence with a difference. Here, we come to the issue of power. Power, any kind of power in fact, means violence. But it is such violence that people have to accept for certain reasons. Clearly, we cannot afford to ignore all these issues.

And the final point. I cannot go along with the suggestion that there are human principles and values on one side, and class approaches on the other. That's not a well-thought-out proposition. Indeed, it was Marxism that, in philosophical terms, first urged protection of human values which were trampled underfoot by the old system.

(*Amity*, October 1988)

7

Tolstoy, Gandhi and India

Chidambara Raghunathan

Tolstoy was Gandhi's political Guru. Tolstoy's famous letter to a "Hindoo" played a significant role in the liberation of India. He was the first to conceive the thesis of non-violence. The weapon of Hartal adopted by Bapuji was born out of this thesis. Tolstoy wrote: "If a man lives only in accord with the law of love, which includes non-resistence and does not participate in any form of violence, not only hundreds will not enslave millions but even millions will be unable to enslave one individual." —Editor

It may be said that of all the great Russian writers and thinkers, it was Leo Tolstoy who first won great admiration, love and popularity among the Indian reading public even at the turn of this century.

India's Friend

It was quite natural because Tolstoy evinced unflagging interest in the problems of India even very earlier. For instance, he followed with interest and sympathy the events of 1857, when Indians waged a massive struggle for independence against the British colonialists. He wrote about the British atrocities in Delhi and elsewhere with bitterness and anger. Moreover, even at the end of the 19th century, Tolstoy reacted keenly to the unbridled colonial brigandage throughout the world. All the greater was his sympathy with regard to the struggle of the Indian people for freedom and independence. It may be recalled here that the Soviet scholar A. Shifman had noted that Swami Vivekananda, who may be rightly mentioned as one of the inspirers of militant nationalism in India, "while travelling in Europe in 1900, intended to visit Yasnaya Polyana (Tolstoy's home) but this trip did not take place".

Correspondents from Madras

Thus, no wonder in that some of the eminent Indians started friendly correspondence with that great writer attracting his attention more on India's social problems. Pointing out the common characteristic of letters received by Tolstoy from Indian correspondents A. Shifman observes: "The majority of Indians wrote to Tolstoy about calamities of their motherland in the hope that the Russian writer, whose voice was heeded to in the world, would come forward in defence of the Indian people".

It is interesting to note that among the Indians who first corresponded with Tolstoy, there were two journalists of Madras also, A. Ramaseshan, Editor of *The Arya*, a socio-political journal published from Madras and D. Gopal Chetty, advocate and publicist of Madras, who edited the journal *The New Reformer*.

Faith in Passive Struggle

Ramaseshan had written many letters to Tolstoy. In his first letter written as far as back in 1901 itself, he observed, "it may, perhaps, surprise you to learn that your name is quite familiar to most of the educated section of my countrymen". After describing the ever increasing weight of British oppression in India, Ramaseshan concluded his first letter to Tolstoy with a request "to give us an encouraging word or two", which according to Ramaseshan, were to be "received by us with that profound respect, which it is sure to command." In his prompt reply written on 25 July 1901, Tolstoy, seeing the Indian people's salvation from colonial oppression in a determined rebuff to the colonialists, wrote, "you should not assist the British in their administration by violence and should not cooperate in any way in organisation which is based on violence." But the resistence against the foreigners should have been carried on, in his view, in passive forms, by refusing to enter military service and to cooperate in the colonial administration.

When Tolstoy's reply was duly published in *The Arya* dated August 1901, the Madras daily *The Hindu* wrote a spirited subleader on the message of Tolstoy, asking its readers to give their "best consideration to it".

Letter to a Hindoo

Especially when the stream of letters from Indians to Tolstoy increased in 1908 after his celebrated article, "I cannot keep quiet" which condemned the bloody crimes of the Russian autocratic regime, and when the Indian correspondents requested him to write an article about India which prompted him to complete his article on India quickly. Tolstoy's famous "Letter to a Hindoo", which was destined to play a significant role in the national liberation movement of India, appeared. Tolstoy wrote in that as follows: "If man lives only in accord with the law of love which includes non-resistence, which has already been revealed to him and is natural to his heart and hence does not participate in any form of violence, not only hundreds will not enslave millions but even millions will be unable to enslave one individual. Do not resist evil, but also yourselves participate not in evil, in the violent deeds of the administration, of the law courts, the collection of taxes, and what is most important, of the soldiers, and no one in the world will enslave you". The path shown by Tolstoy was the path of non-resistance to evil or violence. But at the same time it also meant non-participation in the affairs based on violence. In short, it was the path of passive resistance.

Gandhiji and Tolstoy

It was this historic 'Letter to a Hindoo' that prompted Gandhiji to write to Tolstoy for the first time, although by that time,

TRANSVAAL FARM

When passive resistance movement was launched by Gandhiji against the atrocious laws in Transvaal, many Indians had to court imprisonment. Gandhiji was very much worried about the families of these Satyagrahis. Fortunately, on 30 May 1910, he surprisingly received an offer, from one German architect, Rev. Mr. Herman Kallenbach, of giving his farm of 1,000 acres with a good house for these families. Gandhiji was also happy to see that the farm products would substantially help in the maintenance of the families. Mr. Kallenbach wrote to Tolstoy that "without asking your permission, I have named this farm as Tolstoy Farm because I have read many of your works and your teachings which have made deep impression on me." Gandhiji also wrote to Tolstoy that "as a spur to further effort to living up to the ideals held before the world by you, the farm is named as Tolstoy Farm." Tolstoy noted in his diary on 6 October 1910: "Pleasant news from Transvaal about the colony of the passive resistors".

that is 1909, he was already familiar with many of Tolstoy's works and ideas.

The correspondence between Gandhi and Tolstoy formed a vivid instance of mutual support of two great minds, but Gandhiji had been taking an interest in Russia, even before he wrote to Tolstoy. In his paper *Indian Opinion* Gandhiji hailed the 1905 Russian Revolution and, while drawing the attention of his readers to the countrywide political strikes of Russian workers, wrote: 'The Tsar could do nothing with them because it was impossible to extract work at the point of the bayonet...This had a great lesson for us. We too can resort to the Russian remedy against tyranny. If the Russian people succeed, the revolution in Russia will be regarded as the greatest victory, the greatest event of the present century".

However, Tolstoy's attitude towards autocracy had attracted Gandhiji and he was particularly impressed with Tolstoy's advice to Indian patriots. It may be said here that Tolstoy was probably the first intellectual savant who developed the thesis of non-violence in a systematic manner and that only from the advice of Tolstoy to the Indian patriots, Gandhiji conceived the idea of Hartal—the potent weapon he later used in the liberation movement of India.

That is why, when Gandhiji wrote later a preface to the English version of Tolstoy's "Letter to a Hindoo," he described himself as "a humble follower of the great teacher (Tolstoy) whom I have long looked upon as one of my guides". The high regard Gandhiji had for Tolstoy could be understood from the naming of the farm he built in Johennesburg as "Tolstoy Farm".

It may be said that Gandhiji advanced very much further than Tolstoy in later years after his bitter experience in South Africa. Tolstoy said "Do not resist evil, but do not participate in it either." But Gandhiji, who remained a man of action, not only plunged into the vortex of politics himself but drew others also into it. It may be said that the involvement of millions of Indian people in active, though non-violent, resistance to tyrannical authority was Gandhiji's major contribution to Indian politics.

The Tolstoy farm is the most important monument of the first non-violent passive resistance movement in the world where Gandhiji implemented the ideals of Tolstoy. In spite of Rudyard Kipling, the East and the West met here on the highest spiritual plane for establishing best norms of truth, love and harmony for humanity. The Tolstoy Farm is the most sacred shrine of pilgrimage for all lovers of peace and non-violence. But today, unfortunately, as the area where the Tolstoy Farm stands has been reserved in the "white colony", it has become difficult for Indians to take care of it. It is in a dilapidated condition with wild grass roundabout. The agencies like UNESCO should move in the matter to preserve and protect this shrine for inspiring the noble mission it has enshrined.

Another letter of Tolstoy to Gandhiji was on 7 October 1910. Here he emphasised in favour of teaching of love. "All the injustice and calamities of mankind have arisen because man repudiated the law of love and replaced it with a law of violence" he said. For Tolstoy's Farm he sent Gandhi and his co-workers his heartiest greetings and warmest wishes for the success of their work, Tolstoy wrote to Gandhiji that "your activity in Transwaal, as it seems to us at this end of the world, is the most essential work, the most important of all the work now being done in the world." Tolstoy observed that this struggle was the first attempt at applying the principle of Satyagraha to masses or men. He added, "I do not know of any historical example of pure mass struggle".

(*Khadi Gramodyog Bhawan Madras Souvenir*, 1981)

8

Galvanising Impact of the October Revolution on India's National-Liberation Movement

G. Adhikari

Tilak had supported the struggle of the working class in Indian politics—he had said so in his speeches to workers in Bombay. He immediately sensed the significance of October. *Kesari*, the paper edited by him, took note of the struggle unfolding in Russia even before the Revolution. Subsequently, as early as 29 January 1918, this paper carried a well-informed article on Lenin in view of the "mischievous propaganda" that was being conducted against him. Several other papers and periodicals all over the country carried articles on Lenin and the October Revolution. Thus, the guarded passes of the Himalayas could not prevent the ideas and news of the Revolution from reaching India, smashing through the security cordon built by the British. Even the Montague-Chelmsford Commission Report in 1918 was forced to acknowledge that "the revolution in Russia was regarded in India as a triumph over despotism... It has given an impetus to Indian political aspirations".

Within three months after the Revolution, in her Presidential speech at the 32nd session of the Indian National Congress on 26 December 1917, referring to the October Revolution, Mrs. Annie Besant declared: "Across Asia, beyond the Himalayas, stretch free and self-ruling nations... . In future, unless India wins self-government, she will look enviously at her self-governing neighbours, and the contrast will intensify her unrest."

In January 1918, a revolutionary group sent a message from Delhi: "Leaders of the Russian Revolution! India congratulates you on the great victory which you won in the interests of world revolution. India is amazed by the noble and human principles you have proclaimed after taking power in your hands." An Indian delegation, which managed to reach Moscow in November 1918 and meet Lenin, stated that the Revolution "has infused in us a new hope and shown us a new way to struggle".

Many of the old guards of the Congress had rejected the imperialist-concocted lies against the Bolsheviks and acclaimed their historic role. Lala Lajpat Rai spoke of hypocrisy and lying of the imperialists and commented that "socialistic, even Bolshevik, truth is any day better, more reliable and more humane than capitalist and imperialist truth". The example of Russia made him see the role of the working class. Presiding over the first session of the All-India Trade Union Congress in 1920, he pointed out: "Imperialism and militarism are the twin children of capitalism; they are one in three and three in one. It is only lately that an antidote has been discovered and that antidote is organised labour."

In May 1921 Lord Reading, the then Viceroy of India, urged Mahatma Gandhi to suspend the non-cooperation movement, under the fantastic plea that the Bolsheviks were getting ready to attack the country. Gandhi replied: "Today there is certainly no fear of a Russian invasion. I have never believed in the Bolshevik menace, and why should any Indian Government, to use the favourite phrase of the erstwhile idol of Bengal—'broad-based on a people's affection'—fear Russian, Bolshevik or any menace?" (*Mahatma*—D.G. Tendulkar, Vol. II, p. 58).

Jawaharlal Nehru clearly understood the significance of the emergence of Russia. In his *Discovery of India,* he said: "...I had no doubt that the Soviet Revolution had advanced human society by a great leap and had lit a bright flame which could not be smothered and that it had laid the foundations for this new civilisation towards which the world could advance." His visit to the Soviet Union in 1927 convinced him that there was "no way of ending the poverty, the vast unemployment, the degradation and the subjection of the Indian people except through socialism".

Rabindranath Tagore had as early as 1918 hailed the October Revolution in his poetic language, comparing Russia with the morning star which ushers in "the sunrise of the new age". Later, he visited the Soviet Union and in his *Letters from Russia* wrote of the "miracle" which had taken place there. October's galvanising impact on numerous intellectuals, writers and poets is undeniable, however much the reactionary agents of imperialism may try to under-assess it.

The October Revolution undoubtedly produced a radicalising effect on the Indian situation from the very beginning. Why was this so? At the end of World War I, India was astir with workers' strikes and massive demonstrations against British repression. Peasant unrest was also growing. It was this awakened India, entering the mass phase of its fight for independence, which looked to the Russian Revolution and to its leader Lenin for inspiration and help. Our people had seen that the concept of self-determination as enunciated by leaders of the West like Woodrow Wilson was deceptive which kept the dependent status of subject nations intact. As against this, Soviet Russia had actually implemented the principle of self-determination, abrogated all unequal treaties imposed on Iran, Turkey and other states, ended the exploitation of and discrimination against the people of the East who had languished under Tsarist bondage, and extended its support and help to all countries battling to free themselves from imperialist shackles. They further saw that Lenin and other leaders of Soviet Russia stood for a new social order in which exploitation of man by man is ended, an order based on brotherhood, equality and cooperation of men, and had established a society in which the working class and the toiling people had come into their own and taken over the reins of administration to build socialism.

The Revolution in Russia gave a new impetus and consciousness to the working class in India, and the '20s and the '30s witnessed an unprecedented upsurge of the trade-union movement with long-drawn strikes and militant actions. The peasantry, too, as in the Punjab and the UP rose in revolt against the British rule and landlord exploitation. The message of October struck a responsive chord both among workers and peasants, and Red Flags and radical slogans began to be raised all over the country. S.A. Dange, Muzaffar Ahmed, Singaravelu Chettiar and S.V. Ghate were among the pioneers who took practical steps to popularise socialism and to build working-class organisations. They became front-rank builders of the working-class and communist movement in India.

The scattered communist groups tried to give coherence and leadership to the anti-imperialist and anti-feudal struggle. These groups united in December 1925 to hold the first communist conference and elect the first Central Committee of the Communist Party of India.

The Revolution in Russia remoulded the thinking of the young terrorist revolutionaries, inspired the students and youth. Left forces dreaming of socialism began to gain ground. The Indian National Congress itself in the early '30s adopted an advanced economic programme, including abolition of landlordism, land to the tillers, and an eight-hour working day and living wage for workers. Under Nehru's leadership the concept of planning was accepted, and the National Planning Commission set up by the Congress put forward the demand for nationalisation of key industries and the building of a public sector. Socialist ideas became popular. India's freedom movement began to be seen as a part of the world-wide anti-imperialist movement.

During the dark days of fascist aggrandisement and the Nazi attack on the Soviet Union, the sympathy and support for the first land of socialism which our country witnessed left no doubt that the gains of October were dear to our people, that they saw in the USSR their friend and ally.

The collapse of the colonial system over the major part of the globe following the rout of fascism and Nazism in World War II was a logical culmination of the chain of events set in motion by the Great October. The victory of the national-liberation movement in India has made it possible in a big way to build friendship and cooperation between India and the Soviet Union. The friendship and cooperation is today an important factor assisting the popular forces in our country to consolidate and strengthen our independence, to overcome the legacy of the colonialist past.

(*Soviet Land,* August 1977)

9

Lenin and the Liberation Struggle in India

E. Komarov

Vladimir Lenin was the first to see, as early as the beginning of the 20th century, the budding national-liberation movement in the East as a new potent force of the world revolutionary process. Therefore, it is quite natural that India, a great Asian country, a country of ancient culture and unusual diversity of social conditions, India which had become one of the first victims of colonialism and one of the first to arise for a struggle against the imperialist yoke, attracted Lenin's attention. He studied several works on the economy and political situation in India, and followed the events of the national-liberation struggle, as reported by the press. He was well informed of Indian philosophy. Yet, Lenin's statements of India are not very numerous. Apparently, unable to make a special study of India, Lenin with his characteristic modesty and a feeling of responsibility, refrained from passing more comprehensive judgements. Yet, his few statements about India are distinguished for depth, precision and, the main thing, Lenin's inherent historical foresight.

Exposure of Colonial Rule

He mercilessly exposed the colonial regime in India. He stressed that colonial enslavement was the cause of the country's economic backwardness and the fantastic poverty of her people. "There is no end to the acts of violence and plunder which goes under the name of the British system of government in India. Nowhere in the world—with the exception, of course, of Russia—will you find such abject mass poverty, such chronic starvation among the people," wrote Lenin in 1908. He bluntly pointed out in 1916, that "Britain stifles industrialisation" in India.

Lenin described the British rule in India as "serfdom", comparing it with tsarist autocracy in Russia. He said that in India "...nearly 300,000,000... are being plundered and outraged by British bureaucrats." At the same time Lenin pointed out that the colonial bureaucracy in India had an excellent schooling and was a potent force ensuring the preservation of the British rule. "The Indian Civil Service consists of about 1,000 persons, a staff of excellently paid excellent officials."

Lenin specifically mentioned the policy of creating differences between the Hindus and the Moslems: "The British rule by means of 'divide et impera'," he pointed out.

Victory of Liberation Movement Forecasted

Realising fully well the great strength of the Imperialist oppressors of India, Lenin nevertheless confidently prognosticated the ultimate victory of the Indian national-liberation movement even at the time when that movement was just starting. He attached decisive importance to the beginning of awakening among the Indian masses, especially of the working class. He had a high opinion of the national leaders whose activities facilitated this awakening and involvement of the popular masses in the political struggle. Thus, in 1908, Lenin spoke of the "political leaders" of the people in India, of Bal Gangadhar Tilak, whom he described as an "Indian democrat". In connection with the general strike in Bombay, in defence of Tilak, in 1908, Lenin arrived at his first far-reaching conclusion about the inevitability of the collapse of the British rule in India: "In India, too, the proletariat has already developed to conscious political mass struggle—and, that being the case, the Russian style British regime in India is doomed!" He wrote this in 1908. And when he spoke of the Russian style British regime, he meant the similarity between tsarist autocracy and the colonial despotism of the British. And is it not indicative that the 1908 general strike in Bombay, regarded by Lenin as evidence of the beginning of awakening of the Indian popular masses and the coming liberation of India—this first major organised manifestation of the working people of India against the British rule, was organised on the principle of the all-Russia political strike of 1905, following the pattern of the manifestations of the Russian proletariat guided by Lenin's party?

Alliance with People of East

In 1917, the world's first socialist state was set up in Russia, a state which from its very inception began pursuing Lenin's policy of alliance with the people of the "East in the struggle against imperialism, for national liberation, social progress and the change over to socialism. As early as June 1917—on the eve of the victory of the Great October Revolution—Lenin wrote that the future socialist state in Russia would "establish a truly revolutionary alliance of the workers and peasants of the colonies and semi-colonies against the despots, against the Khans, for expulsion of the Germans from Turkey, the British from Persia, India, Egypt, etc." Besides, even before the first Socialist State was formed, Lenin quite definitely pointed out that it would render unselfish aid to the people of the East in their development and progress: "We shall exert," he wrote as far back as 1916, "every effort to foster association and merger with the Mongolians, Persians, Indians, Egyptians. We will help them pass to the use of machinery, to the lightening of labour, to democracy, to socialism."

Having become the head of the Soviet state, and laying the foundations of its policies aimed at supporting the opperessed nations, Lenin displayed keen interest in the course of the national-liberation struggle in India which, at that time, was mounting to a new and a higher stage. This fact was emphasised by Lenin in his message to India in 1920. He spoke of the "awakening of the Indian worker and peasants", and welcomed "progressive Indians who are waging a heroic fight for their freedom". He specially emphasised the need for unity between Hindus and Moslems, for the success of the liberation struggle. His message ended with the words: "Long live a free Asia." In 1921, Lenin pointed out India's outstanding role amidst the countries whose people were fighting for national liberation.

"British India is at the head of these countries," he wrote, "and there revolution is maturing in proportion, on the one hand, to the growth of the industrial and railway proletariat, and, on the other, to the increase in the brutal terrorism of the British, who with ever greater frequency resort to massacres (Amritsar), public floggings, etc."

On Gandhi

It should be said that the immense peculiarity of India's socio-political development was far from being understood by everyone. This resulted in distorted sectarian assessments, by some personalities in the communist movement, including those in India proper, of the course of the national-liberation struggle in India and the role of its leaders, especially Mahatma Gandhi. We know now that Lenin was against such assessments. There were controversies between him and M.N. Roy, specifically on the issue of the attitude to Gandhi. Roy says in his reminiscences that Lenin considered that Gandhi, by organising and heading the massive anti-imperialist struggle, played thereby a revolutionary part. Disagreeing with Roy at a discussion at the commission for the national and colonial issues of the Second Congress of the Comintern in 1920, Lenin, according to a verbatim report, said the following: "In Russia we supported the liberal liberation movement during the assault on tsarism. The Indian communists should support the bourgeois—democratic movement, without merging with it."

Lenin's policy was aimed at establishing a single front of all the anti-imperialist and anti-feudal forces in the countries oppressed by imperialism, at establishing an alliance between the national liberation movement and the international working class, and with Soviet Russia, the world's first country of socialism.

On that way Lenin laid the foundations of the Soviet-Indian cooperation which saw versatile development in our days and became an important factor of peace and progress.

(Press Release, Issued by the Information Department of the USSR Embassy in India, 13 April 1973)

10

India's Response to Lenin

A. Vasilyev

In India, just as in other countries of the East, the name of V.I. Lenin, unknown before the October Revolution, soon after it became widely popular. The British colonial authorities were doing everything to prevent the flow of truthful information about Lenin and the revolution in Russia in India. In the words of S.S. Josh, who worked for some time at the censorship department, everything even remotely connected with the name of Lenin or with the October Revolution was prohibited. A counter-propaganda campaign was launched, including the publication of all sort of malicious fabrications about the revolution and its leader. But in spite of that, from the very start of revolutionary events in Russia, the Indian national press showed a deep sympathetic interest in them and, despite the threats of all possible repressions on the part of the authorities, the Indian newspapers and magazines printed numerous articles about the October Revolution and V.I. Lenin.

First books about V.I. Lenin appeared in India in the early 1920s. His first biography in English was published by progressive journalist Krishna Rao in 1921, and soon books in national languages began to come out. In 1922, R.S. Avasthi published in Hindi a book about V.I. Lenin, entitled *The Bolshevik Magician*, and Hasan Aziz Bhopali published in Urdu the book *Lenin and the Russian Revolution*. In Bengali the book *Lenin* was published Toy Phanibhushan Ghosh in 1921, and in Tamil the book *Lenin's Religion and Marxism* was but out even earlier, in 1920. Of course, due to the shortage of trustworthy materials and to the authors' failure clearly to understand the nature of the developments these books had certain incompleteness and inaccuracies. Nevertheless, the appearance of books about V.I. Lenin in the main national languages of India testified to the tremendous interest the Indian public showed in the leader of the Russian revolution and his teaching. The name of Lenin was invariably associated with the ideas of the right of all people to independent development, of freedom, peace and democracy; it became the symbol of struggle against imperialism and colonialism.

When Rumours were Rife About Lenin's Death

No wonder, therefore,, that the news of his death was received in India with a deep sorrow. It must be said that bourgeois news agencies, engaging in wishful thinking, repeatedly published false reports of Lenin's death. One of such reports of V.I. Lenin's assassination in the Caucasus was spread by Reuter early in July 1922. Some of the organs of the Indian press received this news with mistrust. The magazine *Maharatta,* started in Poona by Tilak, said: "The news of the death of Lenin does not startle us. For it is not the first time that we receive it. For us it will not be surprising if we hear that it is false, for we are accustomed to that too. But those who heartily wish that Lenin should die, will have a short period of relief extending from the news of his death of its denial. They have enjoyed two or three such short periods of relief before."

The Bengal newspaper *Ananda Bazar Patrika* also doubted the truth of the news.

Comments by other papers reflected the feelings of admiration and deep respect for V.I. Lenin. The newspaper *Nayak* said: "Which country is there in the present world which has savant genius and philosopher like him?"

When it became clear that the news of Lenin's death was false, patriotic Indian papers expressed a feeling of relief and joy. The newspaper *Yugavarta* stressed that there was no such lie which was not spread about Lenin by European newspapers.

Enumerating different reports of Lenin's death, it advised to be wary of such news. An attempt to analyse the reasons of the hatred the European bourgeoisie had for Lenin was made in a number of other newspapers. The Bengal daily *Prabhakar* said, for instance, on 9 August 1922: "Lenin has declared a religious war against capitalism and will not shrink even if all the powers of the world unite against him."

Tributes

When the true report of the death of the leader of the proletarian revolution came, the Indian press responded with numerous articles in sympathy.

The magazine *Maharatta* in its issue of 27 January 1924 frontpaged the report: "Lenin is reported to have died in the hills near Moscow. The All Russian Council is going to continue his work. May his mighty soul rest in peace.".

In their articles about Lenin, Indian authors appraised his life. Their analysis was not always sufficiently profound and not always they could appreciate to the full magnitude of his deeds. Many of the Indian authors could not understand and accept the ideas of the proletarian revolution and of abolition of the capitalist system. But these articles were invariably marked with a feeling of tremendous sympathy for the great leader.

The newspaper *Bengali* founded by Surendranath Banerjee, the patriarch of the Indian National Congress, said: "The death of Lenin has removed from this world one of the most striking and masterful personalities of modern times—a man who had a large hand in shaping a new heaven and new earth in our days."

Anunda Bazar Patrika stressed that the death of Lenin was a loss for the whole of mankind: "The noble-minded Lenin, the friend of humanity is dead. He was one of those great men who tried to find out the means of deliverance of humanity and entered the field of action even at the risk of their lives."

Friend of Humanity

The correct appraisal of Lenin's activities was closest of

all approached by the first printed organs expressing the interests of the Indian working people. The fortnightly *Workers and Peasants Gazette* founded in Madras in January 1924 by Singaravelu Chettiyar, one of the leading trade unionists in India, expressed the grief of the Indian proletariat. "Today the vested interests which are taking shelter under ignorance and greed are silent over the great loss which the humble workers of the world have suffered by the death of their greatest protagonist. It is the worker, the true salt of the earth, that mourns or ought to mourn for him who showed him the path of deliverance from bondage, privation and misery... To him who has done so much and who has given the workers a clear vision of his glorious realm in which every human being shall have the right to labour and to live like all his other fellows, we lift up our hands in love, devotion and reverence.

Lenin's ideas began to be realised in the practical activities of first Indian communists. In December 1925, the constituent conference of the Communist Party of India took place in Kanpur. Singaravelu Chettiyar said in his presidential address that the world "has grown sadder" with the death of Lenin, that the lies spread about him in the capitalist world were short-lived and that Lenin belonged to the whole of humanity:"...there can be no doubt that the work begun by this man in Russia will ultimately benefit mankind and shower happiness and contentment upon the human race."

In subsequent years the Indian trade unions and progressive organisations regularly observed Lenin Day. His works began to be published in India, and Lenin's ideas became accessible to the wide masses of working people. Of great importance for the Indian public was Jawaharlal Nehru's book *Soviet Russia* published in 1927, one of whose chapters was devoted to Lenin. But the above-mentioned first comments on Lenin's death show that even earlier the patriotic Indian press saw in Lenin the great friend of the people of India and of the entire East.

(Issued by the Information Department of the USSR Embassy in India, 29 August 1969)

11

Lenin and the Indian Patriots

I. Andronov

Lenin is the dawn which dispelled darkness over Russia. He is the sunrise which set us all astir.

These lines from a poem about Lenin, written by an outstanding Indian poet, Mahakavi Vallathol, reflect, in fact, the attitude of several generations of Indian patriots to the leader of the Great October Socialist Revolution. It is no accident that Mahatma Gandhi referred to Lenin as a "wonderful man of spirit", and Nehru regarded him as the "greatest man of the epoch". For decades hundreds of followers of Gandhi and Nehru looked to the Soviet state, created by Lenin, as a friend and ally of the freedom-loving Indian people. As soon as the shots fired by the Aurora in October 1917 resounded over the cold Neva and its powerful echo reverberated as far as India, some Indian patriots, notwithstanding the obstacles created by the British colonial authorities, made attempts to establish personal contacts with Lenin. Who were those people?

Unfortunately, what we know about them are only isolated facts. We know, for instance, that in autumn 1918 the first delegation came from India to Moscow to greet the Russian Communists and to ask for their help in the Indian people's struggle against the British Colonialism. Lenin received the delegation in the Kremlin on 23 November 1918. Some documents dating to that time name the members of the delegation as Mohammed Hadi and Ahmed Harls. But these were fictitious names adopted by the Indian patriots to confuse the British intelligence service eager to seize them. What their real names were we still do not know.

In May 1919, Lenin received one more delegation from India headed by Maulvi Barkatulla, a member of the Indian Congress, and Raja Mahendra Pratap, a fighter in the anti-colonial movement. Along with them were also Abdur Rab and Prativadi Acharya. Among them Raja Mahendra Pratap alone is alive. He is eighty. He is the only living Indian who has met Lenin and talked to the great leader. The author of this article has been in correspondent with Raja Mahendra Pratap for quite a number of years.

The house in Moscow assigned in 1919 to Raja Mahendra Pratap and to his comrades still exists. It is a spacious cottage on the bank of the Moskva River opposite the Kremlin. Half a century ago, this house was usually reserved for the most honoured guests of the Soviet Government. Although Raja Mahendra Pratap and his compatriots could not officially represent their country at that time, they were received with special warmth, which showed the deep sympathies Lenin's Government had for the fighters for India's freedom.

Raja Mahendra Pratap recalls in his letters that Lenin received them in his study with much warmth and talked to every member of the delegation, not forgetting even Maulvi Barkatulla's servent, Ibrahim. This meeting with Lenin made a tremendous impression on the Indian patriots. Maulvi Barkatulla and Abdur Rab later established close friendly relations with the leaders of the young Soviet republic. In 1920, Abdur Rab once again called on Lenin in the Kremlin and helped him to select books on India for his personal library. One of these books—a historical-economic treatise by Lala Lajpat Rai, entitled *Britain's Debt to India*—is preserved even today.

A year after meeting Lenin, Prativadi Act Acharya attended as a delegate from India, the 2nd Congress of the Communist International in Moscow and heard Lenin speak. Along with the Acharya was another Indian delegate at the Congress, Abani Mukharjee from Bengal. This Indian patriot discussed with Lenin the situation in India and problems of the national-liberation movement of his country. I learnt this from Mukerjee's widow, Rosa Fitinhof, now living with her daughter and grandson in Leningrad. Rosa Fitinhof is now seventy-one. In 1919–1920, she was an assistant to Lenin's secretary.

On his mother's side, Abani Mukerjee was related to Rabindranath Tagore. In his young years, Mukerjee join India's liberation movement, but the persecution of the colonial authorities forced him into emigration. However, in 1916 the British authorities tracked him down and put him under arrest. Abani Mukerjee was put in the British hard-labour prison in Singapore. In 1917, he escaped, went to Java, then to the Netherlands, then to Germany and in 1920 came to Soviet Russia. The British Government of India wanted Moscow to hand him over to them to be produced before a court-martial, but the Soviet authorities categorically refused to do so.

While in the USSR, Mukerjee wrote two books on Indian economic and political problems and a great many articles on the life and struggle of his oppressed people. He delivered many lectures on India and greatly contributed to the starting of Indian studies in the USSR.

In an indirect way, Lenin himself contributed to the Abani Mukerjee's embarking on a scholarly career. In 1921, Mukerjee sent to Lenin the manuscript of his article on the Malabar revolt. One of the Moscow's archives has preserved Lenin's note on the article. The great leader wrote that Mukerjee's article was "not bad" and added: "More printing space must be given to Indian comrades in order to encourage them and to collect more information on India and its revolutionary movement."

As we see, Lenin's attitude towards the Indian patriots, who devoted their lives to the struggle for their country's liberation, was extremely heart-warming. Lenin expressed deep sympathy with India's anti-colonial movement. As early as 1900, through the columns of the underground Iskra, he sharply condemned the British colonial authorities for the hunger in India. In 1908, Lenin welcomed the historic strike of Bombay's textile workers. He protested against the partition of Bengal. He welcomed the uprising of Indian soldiers in 1915 in Singapore and vehemently condemned the British colonialists for the massacre in 1919 at the Jallianwalla Bagh in Amritsar. Lenin strongly upheld the belief that it was the internationalist duty of Soviet state to give assistance to all people fighting for their national independence. In 1920, he told an Indian emigrant in Moscow that for him Mahatma Gandhi was the "inspirer and leader of the popular movement" for India's liberation and that he wanted the Indian people to attain independence as soon as possible.

The Indian people won freedom after a great struggle involving many sacrifices. We Soviet people honour the memory of those Indian patriots who fought for the freedom of their country.

(*Soviet Land,* May 1961)

12

Lenin and Indian Revolutionaries

R. Yunitskaya

There were Indians too among the Foreign Revolutionaries who Visited Lenin in the Kremlin

Vladimir Ilyich Lenin, who was a great friend of the oppressed people of the whole world, paid a good deal of attention to questions concerning the national liberation movement in the countries of the East. He attentively followed the course of events in India, where, after the victory of the October Revolution, the struggle for freedom acquired a new sweep and power. It can be said without exaggeration that more representatives from India than from, any other Eastern country visited the head of the Soviet state. Among them were public figures and revolutionaries. Lenin always found time to talk with them at length on various matters.

The volumes of the *Collected Works of V.I. Lenin* contain reports of such meetings with delegates from India. For instance, we read in one place that on 23 November 1918 he had a talk with M.N. Roy.

But it is not only these visits that testify to Lenin's interest in Indian affairs. Two of Lenin's notes, to which reference is made here, supplement the materials we already know about.

On 7 July 1921, during the work of the Third Congress of the Communist International, some leaders of the Indian revolutionary movement, Virendranath Chattopadhyaya, G.A. Lugani and P. Khankhoje, sent Lenin their "Theses on India and the World Revolution", presented to the Executive Committee of the Communist International and the Commission of the Congress on the Eastern question. And also a note in which they requested Lenin for a meeting. "We hope that when you have the time, we shall have an opportunity to talk with you personally about the Indian question," they wrote.

As Chattopadhyaya later recalled, the theses "were politically wrong in most of their clauses. We impatiently awaited that interview with Lenin."

Reading this letter, the question naturally occurred to us. Did Lenin reply to the Indian revolutionaries? Lenin's file of outgoing letters threw some light on the question. In the Central Party Archives of the Institute of Marxism-Leninism there is a register of documents sent out by Lenin. In this register there is an entry (No. 501, dated 8 July 1921), which says that a letter by Lenin in the English language had been sent to Lugani, Chattopadhyaya and Khankhoje. However, neither the original letter nor its copy was available at the Institute of Marxism-Leninism. It was only recently that the institute received information from E.N. Komarov, senior scientific worker in the Institute of the Peoples of Asia, to the effect that L.E. Karunovskaya, the widow of Virendranath Chattopadhyaya, had preserved a report of his, written in German language as he had dictated it. Chattopadhyaya, who was at that time senior scientific worker in the Indian department of the Institute of Ethnography of the Academy of Sciences of the USSR, had made this report on 18 March 1934, at a general meeting of the Academy of Sciences.

In his report Chattopadhyaya said: "Lenin sent us the following lines in English, written by him personally:

'Comrades Chattopadhyaya, Lugani and Khankhoje,

'I read your theses with great interest. But why new theses? I shall speak to you about this soon.

'Fraternally yours,

'V. Lenin.'"

Lenin's original note, which Chattopadhyaya had, as he stated in his report, turned over for safe-keeping to the Bureau of the League Against Imperialism in Berlin, was confiscated, together with other documents, after Hitler's advent to power. The Institute of Marxism-Leninism of the Central Committee of the Socialist Unity Party of Germany is now trying to trace these precious lines in Lenin's hand.

Lenin's intention to have a talk with the Indian revolutionaries was, however, not realised. He was ill at the time and was staying at Gorki for rest.

Lenin's second note, addressed to the Indian revolutionary Bhupendranath Datta, refers to the same period.

In 1921, when Bhupendranath Datta was, in his own words, a young revolutionary living in exile and fighting for the independence of his country, representatives of the Comintern invited him and other Indian revolutionaries for a discussion on the problems of India's struggle for freedom.

On 23 August Datta sent Lenin his theses: "Communist Revolution—Final Solution of the Indian Problem," with the following covering letter:

"Comrade Lenin,

Dear Comrade, I am an Indian who has come from Western Europe with a group of Indian revolutionaries. I am sending you the corrected text of my article on the situation in India and the character of the revolutionary forces in that country.

Various viewpoints have been advanced regarding the essence and aims of the Indian revolutionary movement. I am advancing my own point of view. I would be extremely grateful to you if you would be so kind as to read the article and express your point of view on the question discussed therein.

Sincerely yours,

Bhupendranath Datta"

Again we find evidence in Lenin's file of outgoing documents under the date 26 August that Lenin did reply to Datta.

Lenin was still in Gorki at that time. However, in spite of his illness, he attentively studied the theses received by him, carefully corrected the one sent by Datta, referring him to his own theses on the national and colonial problems submitted to the Second Congress of the Comintern, and advised him to pay attention to the specific position of India as a peasant country.

"Dear Comrade Datta," wrote Lenin, "I have read your theses. I shall not argue about the social classes. It seems to me we should be guided by my theses on the colonial question. Get some statistical data about the peasant unions if there are such in India.

Yours...

V. Ulyanov (Lenin)"

The text of Lenin's note is quoted in Datta's foreword to his book, *The Development of India's Agricultural Economy*, and also in another book of his, *Unpublished Political History*. The latter version contains the additional words: "To Comrade Datta." Neither Lenin's manuscript nor a copy of it is to be found in the Institute of Marxism-Leninism. Quite possibly, the original note of Lenin was in Datta's possession at the time the book was written and it may now be with his heirs.

Lenin's note was of great significance to Datta. In the foreword to his book *The Development of India's Agricultural Economy* he wrote that the note was a discovery for him. It had not occurred to him that the peasant movement was of significance for the movement of national liberation. Lenin's statement to the effect that before discussing the question of social classes, one must show an interest in the peasant movement, made him ponder over the matter and changed his view on the means and methods of struggle for freedom in India.

In September 1921, E.S. Varga, in a conversation with Datta, reminded him that he "should do the work assigned to him by Comrade Lenin". Datta's trip to Moscow and his contact with Lenin helped him to write the above-mentioned book.

Lenin's notes on the Indian question, referred to above, once again show what great attention Lenin bestowed on every foreign revolutionary leader who came to Russia and applied to him for aid, how patiently he helped them to tackle all difficult questions and explained the tasks facing them.

(*Soviet Land,* August 1969)

13

New Light on Bombay Events of 1908

A. Vasilyev

The Trial of Lok Manya Tilak and the political strike which broke out in Bombay at the end of July 1908 hold a special place in the chain of events during the 1905–1908 national upsurge in India. These two events marked a new stage in the development of the anti-imperialist movement of the Indian people and, at the same time, proved that the working class of India had emerged on the political arena of the country. It was not fortuitous that the events immediately attracted the attention of V.I. Lenin, who commented on them in his article "Inflammable Material in World Politics". He called Tilak a democrat and evaluated the Bombay strike as a demonstration of the fact that the Indian proletariat had "already developed to conscious political mass struggle".

Interesting documents on the Bombay events of 1908 have been discovered in the files of the Foreign Ministry of Tsarist Russia preserved in Soviet archives. The Russian Consulate, which had been functioning in Bombay from 1900, sent information on economic and political issues to the Tsarist capital. The fact that the reports were confidential and were not meant for press guaranteed a certain degree of their objectivity.

In 1908, Geiking, the Russian Consul, became an involuntary witness to the stormy events in Bombay.

As is known, Tilak was arrested in June 1908. But Geiking had written back home even earlier that the British "kept a sharp eye" on the leader of the radical wing of the national-liberation movement.

The Consul correctly stressed that Tilak's arrest was not simply an act of persecuting one man. The colonialists had, in fact, launched an offensive against the liberation movement as a whole. "By calling Tilak to account, the Government showed, beyond doubt, its determination to combat the revolutionary movement because it is not without reason that this highly educated and adroit lawyer is regarded here as the father of extremism and the leader of the nationalists," Geiking wrote.

Tilak's arrest and trial were in the focus of Indian public opinion. The Russian Consul was present at the trial and sent a detailed report about it. Besides, he enclosed Tilak's articles published in the *Kesari*. These articles, translated into English from Marathi—Tilak's mother-tongue—were processed on a printing machine marked "High Court, Bombay". At the trial, Tilak was charged of having written them. These articles form a valuable source material for Soviet historians for studying the socio-political views of this outstanding Indian patriot. Tilak advocated through them the idea of the leading role of the people, the idea of their right to fight for freedom. It is worth noting that Tilak often referred to Russia and to the Russian revolutionary movement.

Tilak greatly impressed Geiking. In one of his reports, he wrote: "He is a resolute and intrepid man. He represents an interesting type of ardent revolutionary. Indeed, he creates, the impression of a person of extreme views. No wonder, the British are afraid of his influence."

At the trial, Geiking heard Tilak's brilliant defence plea which is said to have lasted 21 hours with some intervals. "He often completely forgot he was defending himself. Instead, he levelled his passionate charge against the existing regime in India," Geiking wrote.

The Russian Consul's dispatches are valuable for another reason. They give the scholars an idea of the character of the protest movement launched against the sentence passed by the colonialists at the trial. Geiking quoted from the Indian patriotic press, reproducing some of their most interesting comments. The *Bande Mataram*, a Bengali newspaper, wrote: "Go on, Tilak! Your body may be destroyed, but your example will stir up all those under arrest. Your chains will cut into your flesh but, at the same time, they will inspire all hearts in the country to fulfil their duty." According to the Consul's reports, "the press, not only of the extremist parties but also of those of moderates, expressed sympathy with Tilak and criticised the sentence passed on him in more or less strong terms".

Geiking reported of another, most peculiar form of protest. Wide sections of the patriotic-minded Indian intelligentsia flooded the courts, the chambers of barristers and the Indian newspapers with denunciatory letters. One of these letters chanced to fall into Geiking's hands, and he sent it to Russia along with his report. The letter, addressed to the editor of the *Advocate of India*, was sent by representatives of a Bombay underground organisation. It was entitled "The Last Warning to the White Bureaucracy". The letter declared that if Tilak died in prison, his immortal spirit would rouse the fearless sons of India for vengeance. It went on to say that thousands of young men had pledged to fight for their country's independence. The signatories declared their determination to avenge the wrong done to Tilak.

The Consul also threw light on a more serious form of protest against the sentence, a protest which in Bombay took the form of mass actions. Geiking rightly gave considerable attention to these actions and wrote: "The most tangible form of expressing sympathy with Tilak is that of closure of shops, the organisation of national strikes, and mass unrest in a large number of Indian cities." He noted that the protest climaxed in the general political strike in Bombay. The Consul's reports give some new facts and do away with certain inaccuracies. For instance, the number of workers participating in the strike was unknown earlier. But Geiking emphasised that "all working people of Bombay joined the strike unitedly". It is thus clear that the entire working class of Bombay, then numbering 100,000, took part in the strike.

Geiking's reports dealing with methods adopted by the British to suppress this first political action of Indian workers are also revealing. The authorities transferred units of the North Hampton regiment to the city. The Consul observed that their number "proved insufficient to establish law and order". Despite the reinforced pickets and despite the blockade of factory areas, the demonstrators fought their way through to the centre of the city. There were open clashes between workers and soldiers; the regular troops found it hard, even with their firearms, to have the upper hand.

The Consul wrote: "The extremely cruel actions were a sign of weakness. The British tried to intimidate the Indians by the brutality of measures taken against them because they were fully aware that since they lacked the adequate number of troops they faced the danger of being suppressed by the infinite number of natives."

The British press tried to minimise the number of Indian victirtis of the repression. *The Times* (London), for instance, reported that only 14 persons had been killed. The Consul in his dispatches revealed : "According to approximate estimates, 200 Hindus were killed in the disorders. The British, so cautious about human life in Britain, shamelessly resorted to firing here. The extremely brutal rebuff was a sign of weakness." "The Bombay massacre!" This is how the Consul rightly called the violence let loose by the British colonial authorities.

Of interest are also the Consul's reports saying that the Indian peasantry did not stand aloof from the political struggle. He reported of peasant unrest in the Panderpur village near Sholapur where they fought under the slogan : "Long Live Tilak!" This slogan, which the authorities had banned, became the most popular with the people.

The new documents discovered in Soviet archives add to our knowledge of the character of the dramatic Bombay events of July 1908, which demonstrated the resolve of the Indian people to put an end to British colonial rule.

(*Soviet Land,* April 1978)

14

New Light on Old Indian Revolutionary

Ilya Suchkov

Indians who had emigrated to Europe, seeking refuge from the persecution of the British colonial police, were among those revolutionaries from India who met V.I. Lenin in Moscow in the early '20s. Virendranath Chattopadhyaya was one of the most prominent figures of that group. Jawaharlal Nehru in his autobiography recalls that he was most impressed by the intellect of the man, which made him an outstanding figure among the Indian revolutionaries in exile. Nehru goes on to note that Chattopadhyaya belonged to a well-known family.

We know for a fact that Chattopadhyaya came to Moscow in 1921 together with his friends, Datt, Lugani and Khankoje to attend the 3rd Congress of the Communist International. All of them, naturally, saw V.I. Lenin at the Congress. But did any member of this Indian group from Berlin meet V.I. Lenin in private and, if so, what were the impressions of their personal contacts with the leader of the October Revolution?

There is a reference in Volume 53 of the *Collected Works* of V.I. Lenin mentioning a letter he wrote to Bhupendranath Datt, a progressive public figure from India, on the national liberation movement in that country. And that is all: no other indication of any kind. However, it transpired that the other members of the delegation also sent their theses on the subject to V.I. Lenin: the issues involved in the struggle of the colonial peoples for their national liberation were on the agenda of the 3rd Congress of the Comintern.

V.I. Lenin sent to the Indian patriots the following note which he had written in his own hand in English:

"To Comrades Chattopadhyaya, Lugani and Khahkoje"

"I read your theses with great interest." But why new theses? I shall soon speak to you on the subject.

"Yours fraternally,

V. Lenin"

"Some of the views expressed in these theses," Chattopadhyaya wrote in his memoirs, "were politically wrong at some basic points as I came to realise at a later stage. But at that time we were impatiently waiting for our interview with Lenin. Unfortunately, however, we did not meet the leader. Lenin's letter was kept safe together with my books and papers in Berlin at the Bureau of the International Anti-Fascist League. It was a grave oversight on my part not to have sent it over to Moscow. The Bureau was closed later by the Hitler police and all its property confiscated—the letter was thus lost."

V.I. Lenin did not discuss the theses with the members of the group. A painstaking analysis of the archives by Soviet Indologists revealed that V.I. Lenin was very ill at the time. He applied to the Organisational Bureau of the Central Committee of the Russian Communist Party (B) for a month's sick leave and left for Gorki, his rest-place, not far from Moscow.

I happened to discover that a man who had known Chattopadhyaya quite well lives in Moscow: K.S. Ramaya of India came here, together with other revolutionaries, and settled down in our country.

"Chattopadhyaya was the most consistent of all the revolutionaries I happened to meet" K.S. Ramaya told me. "He was connected in his time with the revolutionary anarchists led by Bakunin in London. He lived in Germany during World War I.

"I came to know Chattopadhyaya in Berlin in 1930. We came over from London and put up at a hotel as soon as we arrived. After a short rest, we went to the headquarters of the Anti-Imperialist League at Frederick Strasse. I came there together with Philip Gunavardena, a friend from Ceylon. Chattopadhyaya was very glad to see us, immediately helped us to rent out a private apartment with a most prestigious address at that. "The police are most unlikely to look for revolutionaries there,' he said jokingly. He cracked jokes all the time but expressed his ideas in a rather sharp and definite manner. 'You might just as well have left this letter behind—it's no good—the man will provide anyone with such stuff,' he said when we gave him a letter of introduction from Saklatvala, an Indian patriot who had lived in London at the time.

"Chatto was a true friend of our family, a man you liked to deal with," K.S. Ramaya went on with his narration.

Ramaya remembers quite well the life Chattopadhyaya led, his family background and his relations. The parents of Chattopadhyaya were very well educated. His father was a prominent scholar and poet and held a senior post at the Ministry of Education; his mother was a poet and singer. The parents tried to have their children properly educated and bring them up as freedom-loving men with hatred for their foreign oppressors. News of the Revolution in Russia was welcomed in the family. Chattopadhyaya's younger brother, Harindranath, visited the USSR in 1928 to study the new revolutionary art and the new ways of stagecraft introduced by the V. Meierhold Theatre. He revisited the Soviet Union in 1956 and his poetic account of the trip was published in a book of verse *New Man's Country*. In his poem Lenin the poet wrote about the leader of the Revolution:

... Everybody knows the arm

That sweeps up in a gesture defiant and bold

To bring courage and light, inspiration

And might to those in the fields,

Power-stations and plants that we build.

Everybody knows those eyes,
Penetrating and wise
And the heart full of passion and flame
That plan the roads into the future
We lay.

"The Chattopadhyaya family had yet another literary figure in their midst. It was Sarojini Naidu, the revolutionary's sister," K.S. Ramaya continued his story. "She was also one of the leaders of the national liberation movement in India.

"And do you know that the widow of the late revolutionary, Lidiya Eduardovna Karunovskaya, lives in Leningrad now." K.S. Ramaya asked me. "She is the one to tell you more about Chatto, I am sure."

Some time later, when I was on an assignment in Leningrad, I did not miss the chance and went to see the lady at the address he had given me. The door bell was answered by a tall, attractive woman who was no longer in her young years. She invited me to enter the house and said: 'That is the place Chattopadhyaya lived in of late."

Some of the personal effects of Chattopadhyaya were given by the widow to the Georgi Dmitrov Museum (in the German Democratic Republic) named after and dedicated to the memory of this outstanding Bulgarian communist and leader of the international communist movement. The Memorial Museum was opened in the former Leipzig City Hall where the ill-famed trial of Dmitrov and several German communists was staged by the Nazis. A whole section of the Leipzig Museum is dedicated to Chattopadhyaya who, for a number of years, was closely associated with Dmitrov.

L.E. Karunovskaya was visited by the representatives of the Berlin Academy of Sciences who came specially to Leningrad to ask her for the personal effects of the revolutionary.

"Chatto, as we called Chattopadhyaya in a friendly way," said Lidiya Karunovskaya, a former research worker of the Institute of Ethnography of the Academy of Sciences of the

USSR in Leningrad, "appeared at our institute in 1933. Our country was passing through a difficult period at the time; even the staple foodstuffs were still rationed. Lodgings were extremely difficult to come by. Sergei Mironovitch Kirov was very helpful in helping the Indian scholar to get settled in Leningrad.

"Virendranath Chattopadhyaya joined the staff of the Indian Department of the Institute. Chatto was a well-read man with a very good command over English, French and German. He knew a number of languages spoken in India. His command over Russian was yet rather poor and, as our rooms at the institute were close by, he often consulted me on the phrasing of the papers he was to submit. That was the beginning of our friendship. Before long, he was appointed the Head of the Department of India, Indonesia and Far East, and as I specialised in Indonesia we co-authored several papers."

L.E. Karunovskaya showed me the *Problems of the Pre-Class Society*—a collection of articles published in connection with the 50th anniversary of Engels' book *Origin of Family, Private Property and State*. One of the articles in the collection was written by Karunovskaya and Chattopadhyaya.

In addition to his research work, Chattopadhyaya devoted much time and energy to teaching. I see an identification card that testifies that "the bearer of this is employed as an Associate Professor of the Leningrad Institute of Oriental Studies named after A.S. Enukidze". The card has an official issue number 159, and is dated 21 February 1935. L.E. Karunovskaya showed me his papers, manuscripts, letters addressed to her. I was most interested in the reminiscences of Chattopadhyaya written by A. Dalsky, a former research worker of the Institute of Ethnography.

"V. Chattopadhyaya, a philologist by education but a newspaperman by profession," A. Dalsky writes, "when still a student, chose the thorny path of a revolutionary devoting his life to the struggle against British imperialism to liberate his native land—India.

"Reprisals were not long in coming and Chattopadhyaya was sentenced to a long-term in jail but escaped to France and then moved to Germany where he was granted political asylum and lived there till 1933."

We learn from notes that Chattopadhyaya was a member of the Communist Party of Germany. While in Berlin, he took active part in the activities of the communist movement with Dmitrov as his immediate superior. At that time, he carried on correspondence with Nehru.

When, in 1933, the Nazis took over in Germany and began making short shrift of the communist movement, Chattopadhyaya was compelled to leave Germany in a hurry and he came to live in the Soviet Union.

He joined one of the sections of the Comintern in Moscow and was then recommended to take up permanent employment in Leningrad at the Institute of Ethnography.

The International Agency of Aid to the Fighters of Revolution, by established tradition, observed its day on the anniversary of the Paris Commune. Chattopadhyaya was invited to deliver the main speech at the general meeting of the research workers of the Academy of Sciences on that day in 1934. He devoted his speech to the revolutionary movement in capitalist countries and to the leader of the proletariat of the world, V.I. Lenin.

A. Dalsky has inserted in his memoirs an interesting excerpt. "I first heard the name of V.I. Lenin," Chattopadhyaya said then, "in the summer of 1910. I joined the colony of the Indian immigrants in Paris as I was forced to leave the United Kingdom to avoid arrest. An outstanding figure among the immigrants was Rustamji Kama. A descendant of a very rich Bombay family, she donated all her property to help the national liberation of the country. She was inclined to share socialist ideas and joined the French Socialist Party. R. Kama attended the Congress of the Socialist Parties in Stuttgart in 1907. V.I. Lenin mentions the presence of Indian delegates at the Congress in his first report on it without mentioning their names. Rustamji Kama in her turn told us about Lenin and about the Russian Social-Democrats, concentrating on the stand they took on the issue of right of self-determination of nations. However, none of us understood at the time the historic role Lenin would play in promoting socialism in the future.

"Years went by," Chattopadhyaya went on, "and when World War I was already on, I heard the name of Lenin for the second time. He was at that time living in Switzerland. Then there was the big write-up about the notorious 'sealed' railway carriage in which Lenin allegedly passed through Germany on his way to Russia. When I came to Stockholm at the beginning of 1917 I found a closely-knit international group of political emigres. I asked them whether Lenin was still in Stockholm. I was very much disappointed to learn, however, that V.I. Lenin had already left Sweden for Russia. By September 1917, I had already established contacts with revolutionary Petrograd. Then the Great October Revolution began, and that event determined my life for the years to come. In 1918, Comrade Vorovsky sent me a cable with an invitation to visit Petrograd. I could not accept the offer for a number of reasons at that time and came to Moscow some time later."

Another event in the tireless activities of Chattopadhyaya might be of interest to the reader. To observe the 10th anniversary of V.I. Lenin's death, the Academy of Sciences was planning the publication of a special collection of articles on the life of the leader of the Revolution. Chattopadhyaya contributed an article to the volume on the contacts V.I. Lenin had with Indian revolutionaries. He was so much carried away by the subject that he plunged into archives looking for new facts and documentary evidence. Had V.I. Lenin met any freedom-fighters from India before the Revolution? That was one of the questions he sought to answer in the course of his research. So, he wrote a letter to N.K. Krupskaya, Lenin's closest associate and wife. And this is what he wrote:

"Moscow

Academy of Sciences
of the USSR, Leningrad
January 25, 1934

"To Comrade Krupskaya!"

"Dear Comrade, I am anxious to learn certain facts of Lenin's Life, no mention of which has been found by me either in your reminiscences or other biographies. I would feel very much obliged to you if you could find time to answer the following questions:

"a) When in London did Lenin ever contact any Indians? If that is the case, would you please recall some of the details.

"b) Two Indians attended the Stuttgart Congress in 1907. One of them, a woman, Rustamji Kama by name, spoke in the debate on the plight of the Indian people. Did Lenin meet her personally and did he discuss India with her?

"c) Did Lenin try personally, or through the help of other comrades, to contact Indian national revolutionaries in exile before the October Revolution (and especially in the 1912–1917 period)?

"I am working on an article 'Lenin and India' for the Academy of Sciences' Lenin Collection and need that information very badly.

"I would be very much obliged to you if you could answer these questions at the earliest convenience. You might, naturally enough, give your answers in Russian.

"As you do not know me, I might refer you to Comrade Pyatnitsky or Comrade Manuilsky.

"Fraternally yours,

Chattopadhyaya"

The questions put by Chattopadhyaya are of great interest for us, too: Here is the answer N.K. Krupskaya gave in response to the inquiry:

"Leningrad — Academy of Sciences,

7.2.34 — Virendranath Chattopadhyaya

"Dear Comrade,

"Unfortunately I cannot recall anything on the matter you are interested in.

'There were no such contacts in London if my memory does not fail me: I did not attend the Stuttgart Congress and Vladimir Ilyich did not tell me anything about it. It is most probable that attempts to establish such contacts were made during the imperialist war but I cannot recall it.

"With fraternal greetings,

N. Krupskaya"

The answer did not discourage Soviet Indologists, and they continue their research in the matter. New documents and information that might come to light as a result of these inquiries may not give a direct answer to the questions Chattopadhyaya had put, but they will certainly provide new links in the studies of the evolution of Soviet–Indian relations, especially at its early stage when V.I. Lenin was at the head of the young Soviet Republic.

(*Soviet Land,* April 1969)

15

Progressive Indians and Our Country

E. Komarov

Ever since the end of the last century, progressive public figures and thinkers in India have looked upon Russia with hope and interest. When rebelling against colonial oppression and dreaming of a better future for their motherland, they drew their inspiration from the heroic liberation struggle of the Russian people and, later, from the victory of the Great October Socialist Revolution and the achievements of socialism in the USSR. While studying the revolutionary developments in our country and its social transformations, they looked for answers to the questions of the present and the future of their own country, questions which vitally concerned them. The experience of our country drew particular attention among the Indian political and ideological leaders like Mahatma Gandhi and Jawaharlal Nehru, the great savant and poet Rabindranath Tagore, the hero of the liberation struggle Bhagat Singh and thousands of others who took part in the national-liberation movement. Among them also were the communists of India who even in the '20s boldly came out in favour of closer contacts and cooperation between the Indians and Soviet people.

The upsurge in the national-liberation struggle in India was part and parcel of the world revolutionary process. World events, progressive social phenomena and ideals were always in the focus of attention of the leaders and the rank-and-file participants in the Indian liberation movement throughout over 100 years of its complicated development. Therefore, when, on the eve of the 20th century, the fulcrum of the world revolutionary process shifted to Russia, where in the context of the anti-Tsarist struggle, an unprecedented social revolution was imminent, Russia became the focal point for the progressive public throughout the world, including India. Thus, even in the 1890s the noted Indian philosopher Swami Vivekananda prophesied that future upheavals were most likely to originate in Russia and open up a new era when the power of the common people would be established over the entire globe.

It was also the time when Mahatma Gandhi, who was then waging a struggle against racial discrimination in South Africa, became acquainted with the works of Leo Tolstoy and called him his teacher. It is a known fact that Tolstoy's criticism of exploitation and oppression, of bourgeois civilisation and the colonial enslavement of India and the other nations of the Orient played a revolutionising role at a certain period in history, despite the Utopian nature of his socio-political thinking. Tolstoy's worldwide fame reflected, in V.I. Lenin's words, the international significance of the Russian revolution. In 1907 Tolstoy made a stirring call to the Indians not to take part "in the violence of the administration, the courts, tax-collection and especially that of the army". This forthright declaration is extremely important for India, wrote the progressive Indian newspaper *Bihari* the same year. This message of Tolstoy greatly influenced the subsequent Civil Disobedience Movement initiated by Gandhi. As a matter of fact even in 1905 Gandhi closely watched the revolutionary developments in Russia and spoke to his compatriots about their inspiring effect on India. He said that the all-Russia political strike of 1905 was a great lesson to the Indians, an example of an organised mass action. We, too, can use this Russian weapon against tyranny, he said. The Russian revolutionaries, he wrote, are daring and patriotic; they serve their homeland selflessly, and it would not be surprising if that country overthrows tyranny and attains freedom. He called upon his countrymen to show strength equal to that displayed by the Russians. This is what he forecast as far back as 1905: "Should the Russian people win, their revolution will be considered as greatest victory, as a major event of our century."

Addressing the session of the Indian National Congress in 1906 its President Dadabhai Naoroji made a special point of mentioning the anti-Tsarist struggle in Russia. He referred to this struggle in advancing a demand for self-government in India for the first time in the history of the Congress Party founded in 1885. Speaking at mass rallies in 1906, Bal Gangadhar Tilak, a leader of the radical group within the Congress Party, discussed the "methods of the Russian political movement" and the struggle for freedom of the Russian people who had defied the savage reprisals of the Tsarist government. The International Socialist Congress held in Stuttgart in 1907 heard an ardent speech by the well-known fighter for Indian freedom, B.R. Kama who said that the day would come when the people of India would "wake up and follow the example of our Russian comrades to whom we address our special fraternal greetings".

The idea of an organised mass struggle against the British domination was accepted by the progressive Indians due to a large extent—to the first Russian Revolution of 1905–1907. The fact that Gandhi saw a great lesson in the all-Russia political strike of 1905, Tilak's discussion of the "Russian methods" of fighting for freedom and Kama's prediction that the Indians would "follow the example of our Russian comrades", did not stop at that. In July 1908, in protest against the judgement of the colonial court that sent Tilak into exile, his followers organised a six-day strike in Bombay. About 100,000 Bombay textile workers took part in the strike which was a major anti-colonial mass action of those years. The strike attracted the attention of V.I. Lenin, who called Tilak an "Indian democrat". In India, too, the proletariat has already developed to launch a conscious political mass struggle, wrote Lenin in this connection.

In view of the situation obtaining in 1905–1907, it is not surprising that the very first reports about the victory of the Great October Revolution were welcomed in India as a thoroughly relevant piece of information. Thus, in December 1917, Annie Besant, acting as the president of the annual session of the Indian National Congress, spoke about the Russian Revolution and the probable establishment of a Russian republic in Europe and Asia, as one of the factors which radically changed the situation in India.

In the first place, the Indians justly saw in Soviet Russia their ally in the struggle against British imperialism. A good illustration is a police report dating back to 1919 which said that Tilak entertained high hopes about the liberation of India by the Bolsheviks. Although this went beyond the bounds of actual possibilities, the enthusiasm of this Indian patriot was roused by the anti imperialist policy pursued by the Soviet power which emancipated the oppressed people of the foremerly Tsarist Russia, and came out resolutely in support of the liberation struggle of the people in the colonial and dependent countries.

As far back as the summer of 1917, Indian emigrants in Stockholm sent an address to the Petrograd Soviet of Workers' and Soldiers' Deputies, which said that revolutionary Russia was striving for lasting peace based on the principle of the rights of people to self-determination which the Russian revolutionaries have elevated to the highest theoretical level.

In 1918 the Indian National Congress put forward a demand for self-determination for India, while one of the party's progressive leaders, Lala Lajpat Rai, particularly stressed the fact that the Bolshevik government had liberated all the oppressed nations of Russia. In this way the victory of the October Revolution became an immediate stimulus invigorating the Indian national aspirations for liberation in India.

The very first news from Soviet Russia attracted the attention of progressive Indians. Not only the national liberation role of the October Revolution, but also its historical importance as an originator of socialism, a new social system, free from oppression and exploitation, caught the imagination of Indians fighting for freedom.

Rabindranath Tagore was one of the first Indians who openly voiced his sympathy with the ideals of the Russian Revolution. Thus, in July 1918, the poet wrote that Russia might sustain a failure, but even if it should fall while holding high the banner of shining ideals, its fall would be like the descent of the morning star which, while fading, heralds the dawn of a new era. He asked his country to take its place in that morning march of mankind towards truth...

Shortly before his death in 1920, Bal Gangadhar Tilak claimed with his characteristic enthusiasm that in Russia the Bolsheviks were implementing the ideals of justice advanced in ancient India. Young Jawaharlal Nehru, who was then just entering the national-liberation movement, wrote in 1919 that the "spectre of communism" of which Marx spoke 70 years ago was incarnated in Russia. Political freedom alone, he added, will not be sufficient for India, social transformations will also be needed.

Categorically dismissing revolutionary violence, Mahatma Gandhi's reaction to Bolshevism was at first negative. However, in 1924 he spoke with satisfaction about the drawing of workers and peasants into the management of the state in the Soviet Union. Moreover, in 1928 he wrote that one could not doubt the fact that the ideal of the Bolsheviks was corroborated by numerous cases of sheer self-sacrifice on the part of men and women; the ideal sanctified by the self-sacrifice of such great souls as Lenin could not be futile.

There were no mass organisations of the working people in India before the victory of the October Revolution in Russia: trade unions were practically non-existent, not to mention peasant organisations.

A different trend became obvious in the speeches of Tilak and other progressive national leaders in the first years after the victorious October Revolution, which, unlike any other world event, emphasised the active role of the workers and peasants.

In 1918, under the leadership of Mahatma Gandhi, textile workers of Ahmedabad went on strike. This was the first major action of this kind in the country. Then, the wave of strike engulfed India, the number of strikers reaching 600,000 at the peak year of 1921. Trade unions were coming into being one after the other all over the country and in 1920 the All-India Trade Union Congress was formed. More than a hundred trade unions joined the Congress or declared their support for it. Addressing the first session of the AITUC, its president Lala Lajpat Rai said, in particular, that the Indian workers had united in order not only to stand up for their interests, but also to establish contacts with the international fraternity of workers in whose vanguard were Russian workers.

Thus, if the first Russian Revolution of 1905 to 1907 promoted among the progressive Indian public the idea of a mass liberation struggle, the victory of the October Revolution stimulated the setting-up of mass organisations of the working people in India for defending their interests. This proved to be a decisive condition for the development of the organised mass national-liberation movement and its final triumph.

At the same time the October Revolution and the upsurge of the organised labour movement it had inspired in India led the advanced activists of the national-liberation struggle to the ideas of scientific socialism. Such young freedom fighters as M.N. Roy, Virendranath Chattopadhyaya, Shripad Amrit Dange, Muzaffar Ahmad and others set out in the years immediately after the October Revolution, to study and propagate these ideas.

The activities of the communists played a very important role in bringing about mass organisations of the working people, and in the development of progressive social trends in the Indian national-liberation movement and in the international contacts. Thus, back in 1921 the communists called upon the Indian National Congress to make the demands of the trade unions and peasant organisations their own. This, they pointed out, will give the Congress firm support of the entire people who are consciously fighting for their interests. In 1923 S.A. Dange published *The Socialist*, the first Marxist journal in India.

The Indian patriots who advanced to the positions of scientific socialism visited "Red Moscow", established contacts with the emerging world communist movement and took part in the activities of the Comintern. In 1925 the Communist Party of India was formed. Protecting the interests of the working people and organising them, the Indian communists took a firm stand with regard to British imperialism and, inspired by the ideas of socialism and proletarian internationalism, were in the vanguard of the liberation struggle.

On 21 January 1930, the sixth anniversary of Lenin's death, Bhagat Singh, a hero of the liberation movement, and his two comrades, members of the Indian Socialist Republican Association, were sentenced to death. On that very day the accused sent a telegram to Moscow which said: On Lenin Day we are sending our heartfelt congratulations to all who are working for the realisation of the ideas of the great Lenin. We wish success to the great experiment that Russia is making. We join our voices to the voice of the world workers' movement. The proletariat will win. Capitalism will be defeated. Death to imperialism!

It was precisely due to the fact that the growing communist movement and its ideals served as an important stimulus heightening the national-liberation struggle that the colonial authorities went out of their way to suppress it and banned the Communist Party for almost 30 years. They seemed to scent Bolshevism everywhere.

The impact of the world's first socialist country became even greater, as did the sympathy for it, when socialist construction in the Soviet Union started showing results. The solution of national question, as well as the progress of the economy and culture in the republics of the Soviet East, had and still has special significance for India. A very good illustration of this is what Jawaharlal Nehru wrote on the eve of India's independence that the main thing for Indians was the example of the Soviet Union which, within the span of only two decades, full of wars and civil strife, and despite the seemingly insurmountable difficulties, achieved colossal success. While communism was not an attraction, he went on, that for all, all were fascinated by the success it had achieved in the field of education, culture, health services and physical education, as well as in solving the problem of nationalities by the brilliant and tremendous effort to create a universe on the ruins of the old...

Rabindranath Tagore, who visited the Soviet union in 1932 and remained its friend till his death, also mentions this in his famous *Rashiyor Chitthi* (Letters From Russia).

Just a few days after his arrival in the USSR, Tagore wrote that, having discarded the bonds of oppression, the workers and peasants straightened themselves and held up their heads. The sight filled him with wonder and joy. Witnessing the process of industrialisation in the Soviet Union, Tagore wrote that industrialisation here did not help the local or foreign capitalists to rake in profits, for the enterprises in Russia belonged exclusively to the people.

Soviet achievements boosted the belief of progressive-minded Indians in the possibility of a national renaissance for their country. Jawaharlal Nehru told the 1936 session of the Indian National Congress that if the future held a great deal of promise for India, it was to a large extent due to Soviet Russia and what it had accomplished.

Before the victory of the October Revolution, India's national leaders, even those who criticised the bourgeois civilisation, could not conceive of the future socio-economic development of their country proceeding on any other basis than that of private enterprise. Mahatma Gandhi rejected the setting up of the modern economy for he was also unable to foresee its being other than capitalist. It took the October Revolution and the subsequent achievements of the USSR to acquaint India with a different approach to the problems of national, economic and social development. At the Indian National Congress session in 1922 the first Indian communists came up with a programme providing for the abolition of the landlord property rights, the nationalisation of municipal services and other democratic measures. In 1931 the Congress declared that in independent India the key branches of industry, as well as transport and mineral resources, would be owned or controlled by the state.

Beginning in the '20s, and especially in '30s, the priority development of the state sector and the introduction of planning became the subject of discussion on the ways of improving the national economy. These questions were discussed not only by those who adhered to the ideas of scientific socialism, but also by the broader strata of the Indian liberation movement.

That this approach, which is the only realistic way of handling the task of the national economic development, was accepted in India was obviously due to the influence of the Soviet achievements and the growth of the progressive forces in Indian society. In evaulating the implications for India of the Soviet effort in economic and cultural development, Jawaharlal Nehru wrote in 1929: If Russia finds a satisfactory solution to these problems, our task in India will be simpler.

Following Mahatma Gandhi, who in 1905 asked the Indian patriots to learn a lesson from the revolutionary events in Russia for launching the mass liberation struggle in India, Jawaharlal Nehru spoke about the important example offered by our country's policy in developing the economy and culture. The problems we face in India, he said, are similar to those Russia encountered some time ago, and they can be solved in the same way the Russians have solved them.

This belief in the strength of our country and its people has been characteristic of the progressive Indians ever since the time Vivekananda and Gandhi made their statements on the eve of the 20th century; it became firm still as the socialist construction proceeded in the USSR. During World War I the leading national organisations and public figures in India declared the support and admiration for the heroic struggle and courage of the Soviet people. They stressed the world-wide historical significance of the first socialist revolution as the defender of the exploited and the oppressed all over the world.

(*Soviet Land,* June 1979)

16

Pioneers of India's Liberation Movement Acclaimed the October Revolution

V.M. Kaul

"Swaraj is my birthright, and I will have it"—this ringing pronouncement of Bal Gangadhar Tilak, which echoed and re-echoed through the length and breadth of the country, galvanised the suppressed masses of India and roused them to a new national consciousness. It was Tilak who first drew the people into the struggle for liberation. The era of appeals and petitions and exhortations to the British rulers had ended and a new epoch of mass action dawned on the Indian scene.

As early as 1908, Lenin saw in the general strike of Bombay textile workers in protest against the arrest of Tilak a portent of the future. An impetuous and passionate lover of his country, a staunch and implacable fighter wedded to struggle against foreign exploitation, how could Tilak remain unmoved when the shackles of feudal and capitalist thraldom were being sundered in Russia by the October Revolution? He considered the Revolution as the "finest triumph" of World War I. Tilak was in London in 1918 and it has now been revealed from archive documents that he held that the victory of the Russian Revolution would greatly help the Indian freedom movement. Later developments in the history of India fully confirmed it.

Tilak's acclamation of October was not merely the result of an emotional reaction. He was well aware of the issues involved. The paper, *Kesari,* which he edited, took note of the struggle unfolding in Russia even before the Revolution. An editorial article, which bears unmistakable signs of Tilak's style, appeared in this paper on 29 January 1918.

It gave the main facts of Lenin's life in view of the "mischievous propaganda" that was being " conducted against him. *Kesari* continued to carry articles on the struggles of European workers against exploitation and for "replacing rich men's rule by a rule of the poor". It hailed the labour strikes in Bombay and castigated the government and the millowners "for raising the bogey of Bolshevism".

The British rulers of India had taken stringent measures to seal off India from the rest of the world and to prevent infiltration of news of the historic developments taking place in Russia But as Prof. Hiren Mukherjee has so graphically said: "in spite of our obscurantists and the then imperialist grip of Britain over us, the guarded passes of the Himalayas could not keep out ideas to which Lenin, preeminently, had given wing by the Revolution of which he was the philosopher and guide."

The ruling passion in India then was the urge for freedom, and a blow struck for emancipation in any part of the world was bound to inspire the patriots. Such a blow was struck in Russia in November 1917. Its reverberations were distinctly felt in India. Even the Montagu-Chelmsford Commission report in 1918 admitted: "The revolution in Russia was regarded in India as a triumph over despotism .... It has given an impetus to Indian political aspirations."

The Russian Revolution had inscribed on its banner the slogan of self-determination of nationalities. India had been demanding the same right from the imperialists, a demand which was met by bullets and persecution. Mrs. Annie Besant, a foreigner who had made India her home and India's deliverance from the White yoke her own cause, within two months of the event, saw the tremendous significance of this aspect of the Revolution. In her presidential speech at the 32nd session of the Indian National Congress, which met in Calcutta on 26 December 1917, she pointed out: "... the Russian Revolution and the probable rise of a Russian republic in Europe and Asia have all changed the conditions existing in India. Across Asia, beyond the Himalayas, stretch free and self-ruling nations ... In future, unless India wins self-government, she will look enviously at her self-governing neighbours, and the contrast will intensify her unrest."

The British, however, strained every nerve to suppress the facts of this contrast and to spread malicious lies about the Revolution. The mouthpieces of the imperialists, in particular, the *Pioneer,* the *Civil and Military Gazette* and the *Statesman,* carried on a virulent campaign against the socialist regime.

It was Lala Lajpat Rai, the Lion of Punjab, a towering, figure, to India's national life at that time, who lashed out at them in no uncertain terms: "When we read the attacks delivered by the hypocritical nations against the Bolsheviks, especially in the columns of the *Pioneer* and the *Civil and Military Gazette,* it surprises us to find that there is no limit to the hypocrisy and lying indulged in by them." And again: "My own experience of Europe and America leads me to think that socialistic, even Bolshevik, truth is any day better, more reliable and more human than capitalist and imperialist truth." Lajpat Rai observed with satisfaction that "the Bolshevik government liberated all the nations under subjection to Russia". He had no doubt been inspired by the establishment of workers' rule in Russia. Presiding over the first session of the All-India Trade Union Congress in 1920, he declared: "Imperialism and militarism are the twin children of capitalism; they are one in three and three in one. It is only lately that an antidote has been discovered and that antidote is organised labour!"

What concretely did workers' rule mean? Bipin Chandra Pal, another stalwart of the Indian national movement, explained this at a meeting in Calcutta on 12 December 1919 "...the Bolsheviks are against all economic and capitalist exploitation and speculation. They are also against all inherited wealth and social precedence."

Deshbandhu Chittaranjan Das the beloved leader not only of Bengal but of the whole of India, was stirred by the October Revolution, and he too became an advocate of the unity and organisation of the working class and actively worked to achieve this, much to the annoyance of the British, as their secret reports which have recently come to light reveal.

As early as 1919, Gandhi, the undisputed leader of the national movement, had exclaimed: "I have never believed in a Bolshevik menace." Later, in 1928, in his paper *Young India,* he made a more positive reference to the developments in the Soviet Union, despite his belief in peaceful methods: "Bolshevism ... aims at the abolition of the institution of private property. This is only an application of the ethical ideal of non-possession in the realm of economics, and if the people adopted this ideal of their own accord or could be made to accept it by means of peaceful persuasion, there could be nothing like it ... There is no questioning the fact that the Bolshevik ideal has behind it the purest sacrifice of countless men and women who have given up their all for its sake, an ideal that is sanctified by sacrifices of such master-spirits as Lenin cannot go in vain, the noble example of their renunciation will be emblazoned for ever and quicken and purify the ideal as time passes."

Motilal Nehru, Gandhi's brilliant lieutenant who carried on a ceaseless struggle against British rule even inside the legislative chambers, was a practical politician. He had not studied the theoretical implications of the October Revolution. He was, however, greatly impressed by its policy of peace and when he visited the Soviet Union in 1927, he realised how unjustifiably it was being maligned by the imperialists. On the floor of the Legislative Assembly, on 14 September 1928, he had occasion to expose the falsehood that was being propagated against the land of Soviets. In his speech opposing the Public Safety (Removal from India) Bill, which was, a calculated move to suppress the spread of communist ideas in India, he denounced the talk of unsavoury Soviet doings and Soviet terror. He spoke of the freedom of religion in the Soviet Union which he had seen for himself. He laid bare how anti-Russian news was "manufactured" and quoted extensively and approvingly from the report of a delegation representing workers' organisations in England and Scotland which had toured the Soviet Union and which had made very favourable and balanced comments on various aspects of life in that country.

It was, of course, Motilal Nehru's illustrious son, Jawaharlal, on whom the October Revolution made the deepest impact and who best understood, as a progressive thinker and historian, the true significance of this momentous event.

In his writings and speeches he made innumerable references to the Soviet Union. We can quote only a few of them to illustrate the point. Thus, in his *Discovery of India,* he wrote: "... I had no doubt that the Soviet Revolution had advanced human society by a great leap and had lit a bright flame which could not be smothered and that it had laid the foundations for that new civilisation towards which the world could advance." Further: "The Russian example shows how a people can revitalise itself, become youthful again, if it is prepared to pay the price for it, and tap the springs of suppressed strength and energy among the masses." In his Autobiography, he pointed out: "While the rests of the world was in the grip of the depression and going backward in some ways, in the Soviet country a great new world was being built up before our eyes. Russia, following the great Lenin, looked into the future and thought of what was to be, while other countries lay numbed under the dead hand of the past and spent their energy in preserving the useless relics of a bygone age. In particular, I was impressed by the reports of the great progress made by the backward regions of Central Asia under the Soviet regime." For him it was "a bright and heartening phenomenon in a dark and dismal world".

Speaking of Lenin in his *Glimpses of World History,* Nehru declared: "... he lives, not in monuments or pictures, but in the mighty work he did, and in the hearts of hundreds of millions of workers today who find inspiration in his example, and the hope of a better day." At another place in his *History*, he stated: "A great nation, Russia, as well as the other parts of the Soviet Union, have made Marx their major prophet, and in the world's great distress today many people, in search of remedies look to him for possible inspiration." Nehru's visit to the Soviet Union in 1927 convinced him that there was "no way of ending the poverty, the vast unemployment, the degradation and the subjection of the Indian people except through socialism."

Subhash Chandra Bose who stirred the youth of India as few men have, noted with satisfaction that "Communism, as it has been expressed in the writings of Marx and Lenin and in the official statements of policy of the Communist International, gives full support to the struggle of national independence and recognise this as an integral part of its world outlook".

The ardent and dauntless revolutionary Bhagat Singh, sent to the gallows by the British, found in the works of Lenin and in books about Russia answers to many burning questions. While undergoing trial, he and his comrades appeared in court on 21 January 1930, the death anniversary of Lenin, wearing red scarves. They shouted slogans like "Long Live the Socialist Revolution", "Long Live the Communist International", and Bhagat Singh read the text of a telegram they wanted to be sent to Moscow: "On Lenin Day, we send hearty greetings to all who are doing something for carrying forward the ideas of great Lenin. We wish success to the great experiment Russia is carrying on. We join our voice to that of the international working class movement."

Not only the political leaders of India but also its eminent writers and poets, who desired to shake people out of apathy and ignorance and to remove the cobwebs of superstition and prejudice, sought inspiration from the October Revolution.

The most outstanding of them was Rabindranath Tagore, who placed India once again on the literary map of the world and who renounced the knighthood conferred on him by the British in indignant protest against the leonine violence unleashed by them against the national movement.

He hailed the October Revolution as early as 1918. In his poetic language he compared Russia with the morning star which ushers in "the sunrise of the new age". Tagore was not satisfied merely with books on the Soviet Union. He wanted to see for himself the mighty transformations which were underway in the first land of socialism.

At the age of 70, he braved the rigours of a severe climate, the hazards and discomforts of a long journey and the displeasure of the British rulers and reached Moscow on 1 September 1930. He travelled through the country and sent a series of enthusiastic letters recording his impressions. In the first letter itself he wrote: "In Russia at last! Had I not come, my life's pilgrimage would have remained incomplete... The first thing that occurs to me is: what incredible courage! ... How has such a great miracle been possible? The answer that I have received in my mind is that, there is no barrier of greed." Further: "What has pleased me most here is the complete disappearance of the vulgar conceit of wealth. For this reason alone the self-respect of the people has been restored; peasants and workers have all shaken off the load of disrespect and raised their heads. How wonderfully easy has become man's relations with his fellows." Addressing a farewell meeting in Moscow, Tagore said: "I am thankful, truly thankful to you all who helped me in visualising in a concrete form the dream of emancipating the people's minds which have been shackled for ages."

Premchand, who gave a new orientation to Hindi literature, was also moved deeply by the October Revolution. As Amrit Rai has said: "... he did not take long to feel the October tremor in his blood and link up with this new experiment in social justice several thousand miles away, possibly because his links with his own toiling and suffering people were deep and true ... There is enough evidence in his writings of the year 1918–1919 to show how his mind was receiving the impact of Lenin and October." In a letter written on 21 December 1919, Premchand declared: "I am now almost a complete believer in Bolshevist principles." In his last piece of writing, he stated: "The sun of a new civilisation is rising... It has uprooted completely the bankerdom or capitalism. The basic principle behind this new civilisation is that every citizen, who creates something by the labour of his body or his mind, can be a respected member of society. Those who lord it over others on the strength of somebody else's labour or riches accumulated by their forefathers, are worthy contempt."

Iqbal, the great Urdu poet who wrote the song *Sare Jahan Se Achcha Hindoostan Hamara* which does not fail to inspire even now, fervidly acclaimed the new socialist state in an eloquent couplet:

From the womb of the earth
has emerged a new Sun;
How long, O Heaven,
wilt thou
mourn the death of
fallen stars?

If space permitted, one could add many other names of eminent writers and poets from all parts of the country—like Sri Sri from Andhra, Vallathol from Kerala, Bharati from Tamilnad, Kazi Nazrul Islam from Bengal—who all felt the warmth of the glow emanating from Russia after October. One could also mention numerous papers and publications in nearly all the languages of the country which refused to be duped by imperialist propaganda and which discerned the true meaning of October. Not all the pioneers of the liberation movement in India were Marxists but all of them realised that October represented a new social order based on equality, on peaceful cooperative labour, on the rule of the toiling masses, an order pledged to help all countries fighting for liberation and a new life.

(*Soviet Land*, August 1978).

17

October Revolution and Indian Immigrants in Germany

A. Raikov

The Berlin group of Indian revolutionary immigrants holds an important place in the history of revolutionary contacts between India and Russia. During World War I, the group brought together prominent leaders of the Indian national-liberation movement. Virendranath Chattopadhaya, Bhupendranath Datta, Muhammed Barkatullah, M.P.T. Acharya, Khankhoje, Taraknath Das, Har Dayal and other distinguished men were members of the group at different periods. Many of them had lived in Western Europe for several years and kept themselves in touch with the Euorpean socialist movement and with the Russian Social Democrats. Har Dayal, for instance, had met in America representatives of various trends of the Russian revolutionary movement before he came to Berlin in 1915. Chattopadhaya knew the well-known Orientalist, Bolshevik M. Pavlovich in Paris before World War I. The members of the Berlin group were the first Indian revolutionaries to establish contacts with the Soviet Government. Their activities played a prominent role in the ideological evolution of some Indian revolutionaries from bourgeois nationalism to Marxism.

Among the first Indians who proclaimed their" adherence to communist ideas were a number of members of the Berlin group. Among the Indian patriots they were the best informed about the activities of the Leninist Party and the quickest to adopt the experience of the October Revolution and the ideology of the Russian Bolsheviks, At the end of World War I, the following two factors contributed to this.

Firstly, the tactics of the Indian patriots, who had hoped to take advantage of imperialist contradictions and to receive aid from the Kaiser Government in organising an armed uprising against the colonialists in India, suffered a complete fiasco. They learned the fact that the Kaiser Government wanted to use them for its imperialist ends and that their alliance with the most aggressive and militarist power cut them off from the progressive revolutionary forces of Europe. Secondly, they had also failed to get assistance from European Social Democrats. In Stockholm, Chattopadhaya and Acharya were negotiating with eminent leaders of the Second International, but the talks came to nothing because the opportunist leaders of European Social Democrats took no interest in the enslaved Asian and African nations.

Therefore, Indian revolutionary immigrants began to look for a new social theory and political tactics and also for new allies on the world scene. And they opted for the forces of the Left in the international social democratic movement. That was why they found as most reasonable the Leninist stand taken by the Bolsheviks who called for an end to the war, for peace without annexations, and for granting the right of self-determination to the oppressed nations. A pamphlet issued by Indian revolutionary immigrants greeted the Russian Leninist revolutionaries who "have accorded to the principle of nationality maximum theoretical application in their programme of world peace."

It was before the Great October Socialist Revolution that members of the Berlin group had started to seek contact with the Bolsheviks, and this immediately came to the knowledge of British officials. On 24 May 1977, the British Ambassador to Sweden cabled to London that Indian immigrants were going to attend a conference of representatives of various nationalities, including Russians. According to the Ambassador, they "wanted to get Lenin or other anti-British extremist leaders in Russia to support the cause of Indian independence".

Before long, Chattopadhaya and Acharya got in touch with Russian Bolsheviks in Stockholm. Bolshevik K.M. Troyanovsky later described them as "honest and dedicated revolutionaries and business-like people".

The October Revolution marked a new stage in the relations between Indian patriots and Russian Bolsheviks. Although the Berlin group did not grasp at once the true meaning of the developments in Russia, it immediately singled out one aspect in the Soviet Government's policies that was particularly close to them: they welcomed with hope and admiration the documents proclaiming the right of nations to self-determination, peace without annexations and indemnities and a policy of support to the colonial nations' struggle. It was early in 1918 that a special supplement to the magazine *Der Neue Orient* (which published many articles written by Indian revolutionaries) carried "The Declaration of Rights of the Peoples of Russia" and the appeal "To All the Working Muslims of Russia and the East". At that time Chattopadhaya worked out and handed over to Troyanovsky an interesting document, a programme for Russian-Indian cooperation, which provided for joint action by the oppressed nations of the East and Soviet Russia. At one of their meetings, Indian revolutionaries decided to adopt the document and Troyanovsky invited Chattopadhaya to visit Moscow.

His visit, however, did not take place in 1918 because Soviet Russia and Germany had severed their relations. But Indian revolutionaries managed to get in touch with the representatives of the Bolshevik Party in Stockholm, which was highly important for further evolution of the Indian revolutionary movement. Marxist ideas began to make their way into the propaganda literature published by the Berlin group at the time. Chattopadhaya was especially active then; he was going to start a newspaper *The Indian Communist* in Stockholm. A British police report described him thus: "His faith is entirely fixed on the Bolsheviks..."

When the Anglo-Afghan War broke out in 1919, members of the Berlin group found the situation most favourable for establishing contacts with Soviet Russia. Several Indian immigrants of the Berlin group went to Afghanistan *via* Moscow. In the summer of 1919, M.P.T. Acharya, Abdur Rab and others followed a Soviet diplomatic mission to Kabul. Even their brief stay in Soviet Russia gave them an idea of the stupendous changes that had taken place after the Revolution. In December 1919, Acharya wrote a letter to his relatives, which was intercepted by the British intelligence service: "As an Indian patriot and as a man who has lived among the working people of Europe and America for some time, I have full sympathy with the present (Russian—*Editor*) revolution... Russia is now a common country of the common people with intelligent and work-loving people at their service... . It is, of course, only a beginning, what they are making there, but it is a promising and successful experiment... . If this government ceased to exist, then woe unto mankind."

The letter expressed the sentiments of Indian patriots who had visited Soviet Russia.

The Indian revolutionaries also profitted a great deal from their meetings and talks with Soviet leaders, particularly with Vladimir Lenin who, in the summer of 1919, received a delegation of the Berlin group: Abdur Rab, M.P.T, Acharya, Dalip Singh Gill and Muhammed Barkatullah. In July–August 1920, Acharya and Abani Mukherjee attended the Second Congress of the Comintern with the right only to take part in the deliberations. A study of the materials of the Congress added to their theoretical knowledge. It was for the first time that they came across such problems as the character of revolutions in the countries of the East, unity of anti-imperialist forces, role of various classes and correlation between class and national features in the liberation struggle.

These problems soon gave rise to heated discussions among the members of the Berlin group; ideological differences emerged, and those who favoured Marxist ideas further moved away from narrow-minded nationalists. In 1920, a conference of Indian immigrants in Stockholm decided to form two separate organisations—communist and nationalist.

According to the British secret service, Dalip Singh Gill—who had been received by Lenin—Mansur and Verma founded in Berlin the Indo-German Bolshevik Society, with the support of the German Communists.

Of course, the views of the members of the Berlin Group could hardly be qualified as Marxist at the time. K.M. Troyanovsky wrote about Chattopadhaya and Acharya: "Although these comrades have not yet formed a definite social and political outlook, there can be no doubt that they are on the right path."

Under the impact of the October Revolution, the views of the members of the Berlin group underwent radical changes. They abandoned for ever the tactics of plotting and seeking allies among Britain's imperialist opponents. Now they pinned their hopes exclusively on the mass movement inside their country and on support from the international working-class movement. They put special emphasis on establishing workers' and peasants' organisations. They realised that neither money nor foreign weapons would crush imperialism and that a revolutionary army could be trained only through political methods and work among the masses.

The lives of the Berlin group members ran different courses. On returning to India, B. Datta began working actively in workers' and peasants' organisations; M.P.T. Acharya joined the Communist Party of India; and V. Chattopadhaya and A. Mukherjee started to work in the Comintern.

(*Soviet Land*, July 1978)

18

Indian Emigre Revolutionaries in Soviet Russia

Alexander Yunel

The political line of Soviet Russia of rendering maximum possible support to the oppressed people of the East in their struggle attracted to that country Indian patriotic emigres even in the early years after the October Revolution. The first to arrive in the homeland of the October Revolution were Indian revolutionaries who had lived in emigration in the countries of Western Europe, America and Asia. "The October Revolution," Sohan Singh Bhakna, one of the founders of the Ghadar Party, recalled, "had a strong impact on Indian revolutionaries living in the USA and other countries. The Ghadar Party immediately sent Santokh Singh and Bhai Rattan Singh to Russia to make a study of the situation there. Their reports on the revolution in Russia and on the conditions obtaining there had an enormous influence on the policy of the Ghadar Party." The news of the revolution in Russia was received with satisfaction by the leaders of the Kabul centre of Indian emigre patriots, too.

The striving of the patriotic organisations in emigration and individual Indians to get first-hand information about the striking changes taking place in Soviet Russia and above all to grasp the liberation ideas of the October Revolution and find out the possibility of getting aid in the struggle for India's freedom led in 1918–1921 to the emigration movement of Indian patriots to Soviet Russia and to their active contacts with the Soviet government and public. In the early years after the October Revolution, the Soviet territories of Turkestan and Transcaucasia became important centres of attraction for many Indian freedom fighters aspiring to set up there some kind of strongholds for their patriotic activity. "The emigration movement among Indian anti-imperialist revolutionaries, fighters for the freedom and independence of their homeland, to Soviet Russia, which was full of dramatism, revolutionary romanticism, sincerity and enthusiasm," Soviet Indologist R. Ulyanovsky writes, "was made possible only by the strong, diverse and very fruitful influence of the Great October Socialist Revolution on the colonial peoples and peoples dependent on imperialism, who were rising to struggle against the foreign rulers. This movement in India could not be stopped either by the Himalayas, Hindukush, or by the all-seeing and all-knowing intelligence service and the cruel British colonial administration in India."

Early in 1919, Indian emigres started arriving in Turkestan from Afghanistan. Among them were M. Barakatulla, R.K.E. Zakharia, Abdur Rab Bark, Trimal Acharya and other revolutionary-minded Indian emigres. They established close contacts with members of the Indian community which had long existed in Turkestan and Indian soldiers who had left the army. All of them were brought together by common anti-imperialist aspirations and a search for effective means of struggle for India's freedom.

The working people of Turkestan treated the Indian patriots with great understanding. Indians were offered an opportunity for setting up the Indian section of the Council for Internationalist Propaganda (Sovinterprop) and putting out printed publications. It was emphasised in an address "To Our Indian Brothers" published in Tashkent in 1920 that "the fraternal alliance between Russia and revolutionary India is a command of history". Indians acquainted themselves with Turkestan's public and cultural affairs. They attended meetings, lectures and concerts, were present at sessions of the Tashkent Soviet, at conferences and congresses of public organisations, and participated in mass rallies. The activities of Indian patriots in Soviet Turkestan alarmed the British authorities who started the smuggling of agents into the community of Indian emigres so as to hamper the process of their consolidation.

More groups of Indians arrived in Turkestan in the autumn of 1920 in connection with the Khilafat movement of Muslims in India. The *muhajireen,* fellow emigrants who had fled during the Hijrat, were bound for Turkey to take part in the liberation struggle, seeking support from Afghanistan, Iran and Soviet Russia. Shaukat Usmani, an activist in the Hijrat movement, pointed out in his reminiscences that "a considerable number of people who crossed into Afghanistan had placed their hopes in Soviet Russia long before leaving their homes". Quite a few young Indians "also used the opportunity and assumed Muslim names so as to cross into Afghanistan and then into Soviet Russia."

All through the autumn of 1920, covering about 300 miles of difficult terrain, almost half of the distance across the high Hindukush mountains, two groups of Indian *muhajireen,* some 180 people, in all, reached Turkestan. The other groups of Indians, who strove to get to Turkestan, were detained by the Afghan authorities because of British pressure.

A group of Indians, who continued their journey to Turkey, were captured by the troops of the Emir of Bokhara. They were rescued from imminent death by a unit of the Red Army sent by Mikhail Frunze, Commander of the Turkestan Front. Soon, they took part in defending the town of Kerki. At the close of 1920, the number of Indian patriots in Central Asia (Tashkent, Bokhara and Samarkand) was more than 200. With the assistance of the Soviet public, Indian emigres conducted political education work among the local Indian community, in which M.N. Roy, M. Shafiq, Shaukat Usmani and A. Safdar actively participated.

Indians, as they put it, admired the enormous energy of Soviet people in building a new way of life, their unparalleled enthusiasm in the striving to assist in the cause of India's liberation.

In the autumn of 1922, the activity of Indian emigres led by Obeidulla Sindhi, member of the Interim Government of India, was banned in Kabul under British pressure. Indian patriots asked the Soviet government for permission to go to Soviet Russia. Through the Soviet Ambassador in Kabul, Obeidulla was informed that he and his colleagues would be welcome guests in the Soviet Union, where he could stay for any period. Soon, a group of 10 Indians led by Maulana Obeidulla set foot on Soviet soil. Their visits to Termez, Kerki and Bokhara evoked the lively interest of Indian emigres in the new way of life in the Soviet East. "My attitude to Soviet Russia fully changed in her favour after what I saw in Bokhara," Sibnath Banerjee wrote in his reminiscences. Indians were strongly impressed in Bokhara by the incipient transformations in the economic and cultural spheres. The numerous meetings of Indian patriots with the public and religious leaders showed the mendacity of imperialist propaganda alleging that religious and other freedoms had been "suppressed" in Soviet Russia.

From the end of 1921, Indian revolutionary emigres, who had acquired an education in Soviet Russia, started returning to India. After making a dangerous journey, they brought to India truthful information about the first socialist country and the Soviet people's friendly feelings for the people of India fighting for freedom. Their life back home was not an easy one. The British colonial authorities took special precautions to prevent their contacts with the local population and arrested them upon return from Soviet Russia. A slanderous campaign was launched in the press about "Bolshevik agents" penetrating into India, though many of the emigres who returned home were not even Communists.

But the truth about life and far-reaching transformations in the Soviet Union broke through. Some revolutionary emigres, who had arrived from Soviet Russia, established contacts with the radically-minded young people, including members of the Indian National Congress, and supplied them with information and literature on the October Revolution and the socialist transformations in the land of Soviets. Later, reminiscences appeared: *From Peshawar to Moscow* and *The Russian Revolution and India* by Shaukat Usmani, *The Unforgettable Journey* by Rafiq Ahmad, *In Search of Freedom* by Akbar Shah, and others containing truthful accounts of participation by Indians in the struggle against the counter-revolution on Soviet soil.

Those Indian revolutionary emigres who settled in the Soviet Union devoted their energies in the subsequent years to research, teaching and journalism, which enabled broad sections of the Soviet people to gain a better idea of the freedom movement in India and to see more clearly the vital problems of topical interest before it.

(*Soviet Land,* November 1987)

19

Bhikaji Rustomji Cama and the Russian Revolutionaries

P. Shastitko

At the turn of the century Paris, known as the "capital of the world", the arbiter of fashion, with its world-famous restaurants and cabarets, attracted the rich from all over the world; who sought pleasure and amusement there. However, the outskirts of the glamorous city were inhabited by workers who still cherished the memory of the Commune. This "Paris of democracy" attracted all those who had to leave their native countries in order to escape the persecution of reactionary and obscurantist forces for their revolutionary activities.

A large group of emigrants from India lived in Paris. They were fighters for their country's freedom who had escaped the horrors of colonialism and the persecution of the omnipresent British police. The British colonial authorities imprisoned all those who raised their voice for India's independence . In 1907 the well-known freedom fighters Lala Lajpat Rai and Sardar Ajit Singh were condemned the penal servitude. In July 1908 the famous political leader and idol of young Indian patriots, Bal Gangadhar Tilak, was unjustly sentenced to a long-term of imprisonment.

Indian emigrants were of different social origins, religious beliefs, convictions, and social status. But all of them were resolutely against the rule of aliens over their native country. According to British and Indian police reports, Paris became the major centre of the revolutionary movement.

Bhikaji Rustomji Cama was prominent among the Indian emigrants. Young and resolute revolutionaries, including Har Dayal, V. Chattopadhayay, and M. Acharya, grouped round her.

Bhikaji Cama was born into a well-to-do Parsee family in Bombay in 1861. She joined the Indian revolutionary movement. However, in 1901 she had to leave her native country. She settled in London and later, in 1907, she moved to Paris. In Paris, Bhikaji Cama took up her residence in a modest guest house in the Etoile quarters. Russian Social-Democrat M. Pavlovich, who often met her wrote, the following: "She was not very young, of poor health, but of strong will and lively... I felt quite at home with her right away, and soon we became good friends. We often saw each other and discussed problems of the Indian revolution."

There were also many groups of Russian revolutionaries in Paris. They had come there after the defeat of the 1905 Revolution to escape the danger of languishing in gloomy Tsarist prisons, Siberian exile, or the danger of execution. Many Social-Democrats stayed in Paris. In 1908 Lenin came there from Switzerland. Lenin's arrival inspired Russian revolutionary emigrants to action. Many theoretical papers were written and discussions on the problems of political practice as well as revolutionary theory were held in Paris. Lenin and the Russian Bolsheviks inspired all the Paris communities of emigrants, including those from the Eastern countries.

Bhikaji Cama took a lively interest in the revolutionary movement in Western Europe and Russia. In 1907, on the invitation of George Jaures, French socialist leader and an impassionate fighter against colonialism, Bhikaji Cama attended the 7th Stuttgart Socialist Congress which discussed the colonial question. Bhikaji Cama made a brilliant speech at the Congress. In her national dress, she mounted the rostrum with a red, yellow and green banner in her hands. Across her shoulder she wore a broad ribbon with the inscription "Bande Mataram!" (Salute to the Motherland!) written in *devanagari* script. She made a strong and impressive speech. "I stand before the tribunal of human justice," she said, "because socialism spells justice." On behalf of her nation, Bhikaji Cama said: "We want the right to self-determination. We demand justice and the right to govern our own affairs." The Indian revolutionary said another very important thing: "The day is not far off when the people of India will follow the example of the Russian friends..." (Retranslated from Russian—*Ed.*)

Bhikaji Cama knew about Lenin and about Bolshevism, although there is no record of her meetings either with Lenin or any other Bolshevik. After the 1917 Great October Socialist Revolution her associate, V. Chattopadhayay, visited the Soviet Union and worked at the Institute of Oriental Studies of the USSR Academy of Sciences. While addressing a session of the Academy in 1934, he noted: "I heard about Lenin for the first time in the summer of 1910. I had to leave Britain to escape arrest and I joined the colony of Indian political emigrants in Paris. Among the emigrants was Bhikaji Cama. She came from a well-to-do family of Bombay and with her entire fortune she devoted herself completely to the struggle for India's national independence. She shared the ideals of socialism and was a member of the French Socialist Party. I joined that party in September 1910. Bhikaji was a delegate to the Stuttgart Congress of 1907... she told us about Lenin, about Russian Social-Democrats, their views, and about the right of nations to self-determination." (Retranslated from Russian—*Ed.*) Incidentally, Lala Har Dayal, a member of Bhikaji Cama's group, published a biography of Karl Marx—the first biography of Marx written by an Indian.

At that time Indians, including Indian emigrants, displayed a keen interest in Russia. On the one hand, they were inspired by the example of the 1905 Russian Revolution, which, in spite of its defeat, had demonstrated the courage and strength of the masses. On the other hand, Indians, including Indian emigrants, took a great interest in Tolstoy's works, particularly after Leo Tolstoy had responded to the letter of Indian journalist Taraknath Das, having written his famous "Letter to a Hindu" in 1908. At that time, under the influence of Tolstoy's ideas, Mohandas Karamchand Gandhi worked out his theory and practice of satyagraha, of a non-violent struggle against colonialism.

Bhikaji Cama and her close associates launched the magazine *Bande Mataram,* which was distributed in Paris, London and India. Through the pages of that magazine they called upon Indians to wage a resolute struggle against the British colonialists, and to resort to armed struggled in order to abolish the system of British colonial oppression. In one of the issues of *Bande Mataram* Bhikaji Cama wrote: "Young India, young Egypt, and young Ireland, I publish for you an article 'How Russians Prepared Their Revolution'. I think it will be interesting and instructive for you." (Retranslated from Russian—*Ed.*) She also printed leaflets urging the Indian people to rise to fight for freedom. "Three years ago I did not want to hear about violence as a subject for discussion," she wrote. "But I have changed my mind, seeing the heartlessness, the hypocrisy and fraud of the Liberals. Why should we consider it wrong to use violence when our enemy compels us to use it? We resort to force only because we are compelled to do so... Is it possible to live without freedom? Friends, discard all obstacles, doubts and fear." (Retranslated from Russian—*Ed.*)[1] Madam Cama came out in favour of an uprising, which entailed inevitable sacrifice for the sake of a noble goal.

In Paris Bhikaji Cama learned about the Russian proletarian writer Maxim Gorky and wanted to learn more about his works. According to M. Pavlovich, Bhikaji Cama "... once asked me to tell her about the theme of Gorky's famous 'Story of the Falcon'. When I did that, she asked me to get the poem and translate it into French. Some time later I did that too. I remember how she shed tears of joy, when I presented her with my poor though elegantly written translation of Gorky's poem. 'This piece,' she said, excitedly, 'is better than any article or leaflet'.

1. See M. Chattopadhyay, "Madam Cama, A Revolutionary Pathfinder", *Mainstream*, July 1972, No. 8, p. 36.

"The story of a courageous fighter who sacrifices his life for the sake of freedom was close to Cama and her friends who could fully appreciate its implications. She particularly admired the following lines which are full of noble pride: 'The headiness of the brave—here is life's wisdom! O, thou brave falcon! In fight with friends thou didst expire. But the time will come—and drops of thy hot blood, like sparks will blaze in the darkness of life, and many bold hearts will burn with fierce thirst for freedom and light!

"'Say thou art dead!... But in the song of the bold and strong in spirit, thou shalt always be a living example, a proud call to freedom and light! We sing the fame of the headiness of the brave'!"

Apparently, through the good Offices of Pavlovich, the Indian revolutionary and the Russian writer exchanged letters. Most probably, the first letters of Gorky and Cama have been lost.

There is a photo of Bhikaji Cama in Gorky's archives. The picture shows her with a ribbon across her shoulder and a banner in her hands. An inscription on the photo reads: "Resistance to Tyranny is Service to the Deity".[2] There is no date on the photograph.

When the First World War broke out, the French police asked the Indian revolutionary to leave Paris and to settle in one of the southern departments of France. In August 1917, Bhikaji Cama asked Pavlovich to hand or dispatch one more letter to Maxim Gorky. Unfortunately, Gorky did not receive this letter and its contents are unknown.

Bhikaji Cama closely followed the development of the 1917 October Revolution in Russia and hailed it. Her poor health prevented her from continuing her revolutionary activities. Her associate Lala Har Dayal got disenchanted with terrorism. During the war he wrote: "I am convinced that we should start the publication of a socialist newspaper and, thus, join

2. "The Archives of Maxim Gorky", Vol. 8, Moscow, 1960, p. 222 (in Russian).

the socialist parties. Then our voice will be heard much better. Otherwise we shall continue uttering our complaints among ourselves. The Socialists alone are really interested in freedom. All other parties are indifferent to Asia and Asians". (Retranslated from Russian—*Ed.*).

(*Soviet Land,* August 1976)

20

A Russian Revolutionary and His Indian Friends

A. Raikov

Mikhail Pavlovich holds a special place in the history of the development of contacts between Indian patriots and Russian revolutionaries. The hitherto unknown documents found recently in Soviet archives shed new light on these contacts.

M. Pavlovich was the name adopted by Mikhail Lazarevich Weltman in his revolutionary and literary activities. An active participant in the Russian revolutionary movement, he was at the same time a prominent Orientalist. He was born in Odessa on 13 March 1871, into the family of an office employee. Even while studying at a secondary school, he had begun to take part in the revolutionary movement. He was arrested several times for this and subjected to solitary confinement. He had to spend five years in exile in Siberia. During the 1905 Russian Revolution, he conducted revolutionary work in the army. But when the revolution was defeated, he had to escape abroad. He went first to Finland and later on moved to France.

Staying in virtual exile, he showed deep interest in problems of the national-liberation movement in the Eastern countries, which were going through a period of awakening under the impact of the 1905 Revolution in Russia. M. Pavlovich combined his scientific pursuits with practical work and at once started establishing contacts with political emigres from Eastern countries, who were living in Paris at the time. As he later recalled, "Indian, Persian and Chinese revolutionaries frequently gathered" in his flat. These get-togethers were of great importance to them, because M. Pavlovich helped them draw up programmes of struggle and formulate basic demands. In his words, he "edited leaflets for Persian, Chinese and Indian revolutionaries and contributed to their journals and newspapers". "This active work for the Eastern national-liberation movement, to which I attached great importance," M. Pavlovich wrote, "held the whole of my attention".

It was precisely in that period that M. Pavlovich maintained close contacts with the Indian political emigres, S. Krishnavarma and B.R. Kama. He met Krishnavarma, sent his articles to him and received from him copies of the journal, *Indian Sociologist,* as they came off the press. It follows from a letter from S. Krishnavarma, dated 8 October 1909, found in M. Pavlovich's personal archives, that M. Pavlovich had sent him an article on the Indian freedom movement. We have not succeeded in establishing its title, but possibly it was the article "The Awakening of India", in which he had vigorously come out in defence of the Indian revolutionaries, who were being characterised as anarchists by the British bourgeois press. M. Pavlovich wrote: "Indian terrorists speak of a national government, of the need to make Britain quit India, but all anarchist theories are totally alien to them." In his letter, Krishnavarma wrote further about mailing to Pavlovich the latest issues of his journal, and also expressed the hope of having personal friendship with him. Most probably, M. Pavlovich must have quickly answered in the affirmative, because in the next letter, dated 16 October 1909, S. Krishnavarma wanted to have a meeting with him. The meeting took place, and their relations grew closer. In his reminiscences, M. Pavlovich writes that they used to see each other regularly.

With B.R. Kama also M. Pavlovich had very close relations. Her patriotic activities won her the honourable title of "mother of the Indian revolution". During his stay in France, M. Pavlovich kept in close touch with her.

These contacts were of great importance for Kama, because through M. Pavlovich she received more exact information on the First Russian Revolution, its motive forces and tasks, and on the socialist ideas. "Kama showed keen interest in the Russian revolutionary events, particularly the 1905 Revolution, the role of the working class in the movement, and read some literature on the theory of Marxism." When she developed interest in the works of the great proletarian writer Maxim Gorky, M. Pavlovich, at her request, translated the *Song of the Stormy Petrel* into French. "I remember," he wrote, "her tears of joy when I presented to her my certainly poor, yet neatly written, translation of Gorky's poem in which she was interested. This little thing, Kama said excitedly, is better than any article, any booklet."

Judging by Kama's speeches at meetings and by materials of the journal *Bande Mataram* she published, one can see that her association with Pavlovich did not pass by without leaving an imprint. Kama became a vigorous advocate of the using of all available means in the fight against colonialism, and later wanted to be a Communist.

Pavlovich's cooperation with Kama grew even closer in 1910, at the time of the campaign in defence of V. Savarkar, an Indian revolutionary, who had been illegally arrested on French territory and handed over to the British authorities in violation of the international right to political asylum. Kama was then actively campaigning to galvanise public opinion and to secure the release of Savarkar. "Despite her age and illness, she personally—sometimes accompanied by myself—," Pavlovich wrote, "visited the newspaper offices and requested them to incorporate some notes on Savarkar..."

M. Pavlovich's participation in the campaign is borne out by Kama's letter to him, dated 2 August 1910: "Dear Mr. Weltman, Thank you very much for sending *la Depeche.* The French foreign office is waiting for the reply from the British about Savarkar, and I feel anxious about what they are up to."

When during World War I, the British demanded that Kama should be expelled from France, M. Pavlovich, together with the French Socialists, campaigned for allowing her to stay on in the country.

When M. Pavlovich was about to leave for Russia in August 1917, Kama sent through him a letter to Maxim Gorky.

On returning to Russia, M. Pavlovich became an active fighter in the cause of the Bolshevik Party, fulfilling important assignments from the Soviet Government and holding a number of responsible posts. During the time, M. Pavlovich's interest in problems of the national-liberation movement grew even further, and his ties with representatives of Eastern countries, who looked to Soviet Russia for support for their cause, became stronger. As a member of the Eastern Commission of the Communist International, M. Pavlovich rendered great assistance to revolutionaries from India and other Eastern countries staying in Soviet Russia. Quite a few documents have been found in his personal archives on direct cooperation with Indian revolutionaries. He took a direct part in organising courses for the representatives of Eastern countries, including Indians. "At these courses, lectures are given in Eastern languages on political economy, the development of the Soviet political system, geography, the origin of the earth and of man," he wrote in his diary in the twenties. He was fully aware of the importance of this educational work. He further noted in his diary that while the so-called freedom-loving Britain was trying to keep hundreds of millions of their Indian "subjects" in ignorance, Soviet Russia, starving, torn apart and bleeding, is trying to do her best from her own meagre funds to provide an education for hundreds of people from the East. This fact alone proves that Soviet Russia was doing all she could to help step up the process of the Eastern peoples' awakening, of their national and revolutionary development.

These courses made a strong impression on the Indians. Thus, a group of Indian soldiers, who had escaped from the British army in 1920, on meeting with M. Pavlovich, asked him in detail about the course. One of the soldiers, after listening to M. Pavlovich's explanations, remarked with bitterness:

"We have spent so many years fighting for Britain in Persia, Turkey and France, and we have not even been taught how to read or write. Soviet Russia is our friend: she wants all Indians, Persians and Turks to see things clearly and realise their position. The whole of the East will stand by Russia."

In the last years of his life, M. Pavlovich devoted much time to the development of Soviet Orientology. He headed the USSR Association of Orientalists and, until his death in 1927, was Rector of the Institute of Eastern Studies. As before, he was keenly interested in Indian history. In 1925, sharing the authorship with V. Gurko-Kryazhin, he published a book, *India in the Fight for Independence.* The year 1957 saw a collection, *As Friends See It,* reproduce a section from this book in which he described his meetings with Indian friends.

Highly appreciated in the Soviet Union are the services of M. Pavlovich not only as a revolutionary and scholar, but also as a person who has made a considerable contribution to the development of Soviet–Indian friendly ties.

(*Soviet Land,* December 1987)

21

First Mention of Marx in Indian Writings

Leonid Mitrokhin

In the spring of 1872, five year after the appearance of the first German (Hamburg) edition of the *Capital,* it became possible for the progressive Russian intelligentsia and representatives of the working class of Russia to study the first volume of the great work of Kal Marx, the founder of scientific communism, in their own language. The first translator of Marx's work into Russian was a revolutionary who gained renown later and became a member of the General Council of the First International set up by Karl Marx and Frederick Engels.

The Russian translation of Karl Marx's work made available to the widest sections of the country's democratic and revolutionary circles a genuinely scientific-philosophical analysis of the socio-political development of society and marked an important stage in the triumphant spread of Marxism in Russia.

However, Marxist ideas proved attractive not only in Russia and the countries of Europe and America. Soon they started making their way into the countries of the colonial East. In the early 70s of the last century, reports of the First International reached the boundaries of India which was then under British domination. It is a well-established fact now that the possibility of setting up an Indian section of the First International was discussed by a meeting of its General Council on 15 August 1871, presided over by Marx, in response to the suggestion contained in a letter received from Calcutta (the names of the Indians who wrote this letter have still not been discovered).

This fact is of great interest in itself. But the investigations of foreign and Indian scholars have not revealed if any Indian writers had mentioned the names of Karl Marx and Frederick Engels during the life-time of the founders of scientific communism. It was only in 1912, under the impact of the 1905 revolution in Russia which had played a tremendous role in the awakening of the people of the East, when reports of the heroic actions of the Russian working class, headed by the Leninist party, started reaching India, that the first books on Marx appeared in India. The first mention of Marx's namc in India known to us, when even an attempt was made to analyse his ideology, we find in the *Modem Review*, a magazine published from Calcutta. In its March issue of 1912, the magazine carried an article by Lala Hardayal, a famous revolutionary who was Secretary of the Ghadar Party, entitled "Karl Marx—Modern Rishi". Having established contact with socialists in the United States, Hardayal had studied Marxism for some time.

The same year saw the appearance in India, in Kerala, of a book, about Karl Marx, by Malayalee journalist K. Ramakrishna Pillai (1870–1916), which was, in fact, a short biography.

Lying on my desk is a small book of a little over 50 pages in Malayalam. This is one of the early editions of the first Indian book about Marx. This copy of the book by K. Ramakrishna Pillai has been received by me as a gift from Indian friends. In his Foreword the author presents Marx to his readers as a great and ideal man who dedicated his entire life and genius to search for ways for the emancipation of the working people from oppression, lack of rights and poverty. The book describes Marx's childhood, the beginning of his creative activity, his titanic work in setting up the First International, etc. But the main merit lies in the assessment of the role and world-wide importance of Marx's writings. The Indian writer states; "Marx is worthy of an eminent position among the humanists in as much as he showed the poor wage-workers the way to salvation."

"By his great call 'Workers of all countries, unite!", Pillai goes on to say, "Marx not only found a way to the hearts of the workers of the world but aroused in them unprecedented courage and determination. This awakening which began then (in Marx's life time—LM) has never waned but only spread wider and wider." (About Karl Marx by K. Pillai, 1967, p. 49).

The first translation of Marx's *Capital* into Russian in 1872 and the appearance of the first book on Marx in India in 1912 seem to be quite separate events. But a deeper analysis and comparison of these two events reveal them to be elements of the same world process: the process of progressive mankind's turn to the theory of scientific socialism, to the study and comprehension of Marxist philosophy, to the realisation of the indisputable fact that the world can be transformed only on the basis of this philosophy.

The Great October Socialist Revolution meant the putting of the great ideas of Karl Marx and Lenin into practice. It marked the beginning of the crisis of the colonial system of imperialism, and a truly victorious march of Marxism-Leninism across the planet began under its influence. The name of Marx became better known in India only after the victory of the October Revolution in Russia in 1917, and, above all, thanks to the worldwide popularity of Lenin. Lenin was widely known in India as the leader of the proletarian revolution and the head of the world's first state of workers and peasants. It was because of Lenin that Karl Marx, whom Lenin considered to be his teacher, became well known in India soon after. The constantly-growing interest in India and other countries of the East in the experience of the socialist revolution in Russia has resulted in the desire to understand the sources of the Marxist teaching, to study more profoundly the works of Marx, Engels and Lenin.

After the October Revolution, Marx's *Capital* has been issued 188 times in the USSR, in editions totalling over 6,500,000 copies, in 20 languages of the people of the USSR and foreign languages. In the last five-years alone editions of Marx's *Capital* have appeared in Russian, Azerbaijanian, Georgian, Lithuanian, Kazakh and Moldavian as well as in Arabic, English and Hindi.

Not only Hindi-speaking people but those speaking Marathi and Malayalam can now read Marx's great work in India. Works of Marx, Engels and Lenin, and Marxist literature are available in virtually all countries of Asia. They are being studied thoroughly and serve as a guide.

(*Soviet Land*, May 1972)

22

Indian Revolutionaries' Pamphlets in Soviet Libraries

A. Raikov

In order to study the history of the Indian national-liberation movement it is absolutely essential to make use of such sources as the publications of the underground patriotic organisations, which did not fall into the hands of censors. I mean newspapers, magazines, pamphlets, books, leaflets and other propaganda materials. It is precisely in such publications that we can trace the evolution of the views of the fighters for freedom and their links with other trends in the liberation movement and the international working-class and democratic movement.

Naturally, the Indian revolutionaries in exile had the greatest opportunity to air their views. During World War I they set up the European Committee of Indian Nationalists in Berlin and started propaganda in order to get the support of the European public opinion in their struggle for India's freedom. They brought out pamphlets and distributed them widely in many European countries. Dr. R.C. Majumdar, the well-known historian who has written a good deal about India's fight for freedom mentioned only three such pamphlets. But, in various libraries of the Soviet Union we have succeeded in finding about 20 more, printed in Berlin, Stockholm, Copenhagen and Berne.

The writer of the article has also tried to find them in the archives and libraries of the German Democratic Republic. But, the attempts proved to be futile. It was established that the Soviet Union has the largest collection of pamphlets written by Indian revolutionaries. This fact testifies not only to the interest of the Russian public in India's fight for freedom but also to the ties which bound Indian and Russian revolutionaries.

Noteworthy is another fact. Indian pamphlets published abroad and addressed to the European public opinion were written not only in English, German, French and Italian but also in Russian. At least three of them appeared in Russian: *The International Socialist Congress: Speeches and Resolutions on India; Opinions of English Socialist Leaders on British Rule in India,* and a brochure by the well-known Indian leader Lala Lajpat Rai entitled *Deliberations on the Political Situation in India.* Unfortunately, these editions were lost during the war.

What do the publications of Indian patriots in exile tell us? Some exposed the methods of British plunder in India (*India's Poverty and India under the English Fist*); others outlined the aims and objects of the Indian revolutionaries (*Why India Is in Revolt against British Rule*). The pamphlet, *Roger Kasement and India,* which expressed solidarity with the Irish liberation movement, one of whose leaders was executed in 1915 by the decision of the British court, is very interesting.

Taken as a whole, the pamphlets of the revolutionaries are a valuable source of information on the history of the socio-political thought in India.

At the same time, the pamphlets show clearly that the positions of the Indian revolutionaries changed after the October Revolution in Russia which kindled not only hopes for victory in the struggle for freedom but also prompted them to reconsider their programmes and tactics.

There was a time when Indian patriots banked on the idea of getting support from the social-democratic parties of Europe. Now, having compared their activities with the practical actions of the Bolsheviks, they realised that the reformist social-democratic parties were "agents of the subtle and ruthless imperialism of the so-called Western democracies". In the pamphlet, *India and World Peace* it was said: "The empty pronouncements of the social-democratic leaders, who adhered to pro-imperialist positions, were opposed by Indian revolutionaries with the theory and practice of the Bolsheviks: "And the Russian revolutionaries, whatever may be said about their methods, have at least accorded to the principle of nationality maximum theoretical application in their programme of world peace."

The pamphlets help to trace the growing interest on the part of Indian revolutionaries in Marxist theory. Under its influence they came to understand class struggle. Some of them took the side of international proletarians and saw in them an ally of the national-liberation movement. Addressing the revolutionary wing of the European socialists, they wrote: "You, who have acquired publicity thanks to the principles of international brotherhood and collective work, will not leave us in our struggle against foreign exploitation. You, who fight against imperialism and capitalism, will not forget that India is a vast proletarian country and that a tremendous number of proletarians live in it who are mercilessly exploited by the British capitalism... Workers of the world! Give a powerful support to our struggle for freedom and social justice."

The pamphlets of the Indian revolutionaries which are preserved in Soviet libraries are an important original source which helps to trace the roots of the big shift in the outlook of Indian revolutionaries who lived in exile.

(*Soviet Land*, April 1970)

23

A Find in the Archives

(Documents About an Unknown Indian Mission to Russia in 1859)

A. Raikov

Russia's growing activity in Central Asia in the middle of the 19th century substantially influenced both the policy of the British colonialists and public sentiment in India.

Though tsarist Russia neither intended to invade India nor possessed the material means to do it, Britain felt rather nervous of the fact that Russia's frontiers were drawing closer to India. At the same time, the advance of the Russians inspired hope in patriotically-minded circles in India that aid in their struggle against the British enslavers would be forthcoming.

From time to time missions arrived in Russia from India, representing interests of different sections of the population. These people complained about the cruel methods used by the British authorities and sought help. The earliest known mission was that of the Maharaja of Kashmir, which was sent to Russian Turkestan in 1865.

But documents about a hitherto unknown mission which set out for Russia in 1859 was found in the archives. These documents are all the more interesting since they are connected with a most important event in India's 19th century history, i.e., the great popular uprising against the colonialists in 1857–1859.

Anti-British feudal rulers of the Indian principalities are known to have predominated among the leaders of the popular uprising. At the moment when the uprising suffered a setback, a group of Indian princes elected from among themselves an envoy and sent him with a letter to the Russian tsar.

Rao Raj Telasingh Bahadur, the "ruler of Rewa," agreed to make this dangerous and long trip. The envoy carried letters from Maharaja Takht Singh Bahadur, the ruler of Marwar, from Maharaja Sirdar Singh Bahadur, the ruler of Bikaner, and from Maharaja Sawai Ram Singh Bahadur, the ruler of Jaipur. There is every evidence that there had been agreement among them, for their messages were very similar in content and used similar expressions.

The letters bear different dates, according to the Muslim calendar. The above-mentioned maharajas dated their letters respectively the 7, 11 and 19 of Safera, the year 1276 of the Hegira, which corresponds to August 26, 30, and September 4, 1859.

Rao Raj Telasingh Bahadur decided to get into Russia through Persia. He reached the port of Bandar Bushehr, where the British tried to detain him. The local authorities supported him and helped him on to Shiraz, where again it was only the patronage of the local powers that saved him from the British.

The envoy managed to get to Teheran, where the British ambassador wanted to prevent him from continuing his trip under various pretexts. The Persian government, however, provided him with the necessary documents with which he arrived in Rasht in December. Since a Russian consulate was open there at that time, he went to the consul and asked to be sent to St. Petersburg so that "he could lay the Indian rajas' petition at the monarch's feet." During his long voyage Rao Raj Telasingh Bahadur lost all he had and the people accompanying him were arrested, but he achieved his main goal—he established contact with the Russian authorities. It is not known whether he ever got to the capital of Russia, but in any case the documents which he had brought did reach St. Petersburg.

The texts of the letters were rather general and did not contain any concrete proposals. The rajas paid their respects to the Tsar and complained of being oppressed by the British authorities. For example, Maharaja of Jaipur wrote: "Since time immemorial the Russian state has served as a lofty haven for kings and rulers of the entire world. All those overwhelmed by the strength of the enemy have always sought the protection of the mighty court of Your Highness. Now our government too, deems it necessary to ask for your favour."

And this is what Maharaja of Marwar wrote to the Tsar:

"Today, the British Government's oppression weighs so heavily on the Hindus and Muslims of India, and particularly on the descendants of the Emir Timur, the ruler of Delhi, that my pen is unable to describe it. Nor do I have the strength to express the frame of my mind resulting from the disarray and the decline of the Indian people. We lie prostrate like corpses one next to the other on a bed of despondency..."

Evidently fearing that the letters might get into the hands of the British, the maharajas limited themselves to brief appeals to the Tsar, relying on Rao Raj for everything. Prince of Bikaner wrote: "Having commissioned Rao Raj with the task of explaining our case to your government, I draw Your Majesty's attention to everything you will learn from him, either verbally or in written form, on my behalf."

The envoy of the maharajas wrote his letter in Rasht on 5 December, 1860. It contained more detailed data of utmost interest to historians and disclosed hitherto unknown circumstances concerning the outbreak of the 1857 uprising. According to Rao Raj, it was not only planned beforehand, but was connected with hopes for the movement of Russian troops in Central Asia.

The letter read: "When the rumour reached India three years ago that the emperor's troops were crossing Turkestan into India, the British asked the Indian rulers whether or not they intended to act jointly with them in the event the rumours were true. These rulers; including your obedient servant, refused to do so."

The "Brief Outline of the Current Situation in India," which was attached to the letter, spoke even more clearly of the sharp reaction which all the foreign policy circumstances, unfavourable for the British, had caused in India.

Describing the cruel repressions of the British, the Indian envoy mentioned another interesting fact showing that the leadership of the uprising had made an attempt to establish contact with Russia in the course of the uprising: "At that time we, your loyal slaves, sent two or three confidential persons here, but they were detained on the way and had to live on charity."

What was the aim of the Indian princes' appeal to Russia? We find the answer to this question in the "Brief Outline of the Current Situation in India," which says that the government of Russia "ought to protect the oppressed from oppression" and that is why the princes decided to ask Russia "to protect them against British oppression and tyranny". Thus, they hoped to rid themselves of the British with the help of the Russians.

Unfortunately, we failed to find in the archives documents which would shed light on the further fate of the mission.

But the documents about the Indian mission which set out for Russia in 1859 opened a hitherto unknown page in the history of mutual relations between the two nations.

(*Soviet Land,* February 1978)

24

Visit of Motilal and Jawaharlal Nehru to the USSR in 1927

A.I. Yunel

Forty-six years ago Jawaharlal Nehru came to the USSR for the celebrations of the 10th anniversary of the Great October Revolution. He visited the land of Soviets along with Motilal Nehru, his father, an outstanding leader of the Indian National Congress, his wife Kamala and younger sister Krishna. Taking place at a time when the British colonialists were trying to create an insurmountable barrier between our people, this visit was a notable event. But let us take a look at the circumstances that lay behind the trip of the eminent leaders of the Indian national-liberation movement to the USSR.

In the second half of the '20s the interest of the Indian National Congress (INC) in foreign affairs began to grow. That was precisely the period when this party's leading circles started to elaborate the main principles of its foreign-policy course. Jawaharlal Nehru noted that "the National Congress began to develop its foreign policy in 1927". (J. Nehru, *The Discovery of India*, Bombay, 1961, p. 443). The Congress was determining its position towards international problems against the background of a grim struggle being waged by the anti-imperialist forces headed by the Soviet Union against the forces of reaction. It is common knowledge that the role of one of the chief inspirers and authors of the foreign-policy course of the party, and subsequently of the Indian Republic, fell to the leader of the Left-wing of the Congress, Jawaharlal Nehru.

In February 1927 Jawaharlal Nehru took part in the Brussels International Congress against Colonial Oppression and Imperialism as an official representative of the INC. The participation of an INC representative in the Congress was a signal event. The *Pravda* said in this connection: "The presence of a representative of an old and quite influential organisation, the Indian National Congress, at the international congress is of special significance." (27 February 1927).

Nehru came to Brussels as already a mature leader, whose interest in the socialist transformations in the USSR had increased. He belonged to that circle of young Congress members on whom the October Revolution, and especially its foreign-policy activities, had made a deep impact. Recalling this period of his life in an interview given to journalist Tibor Mende in 1956, Nehru emphasised: "The Bolshevik Revolution was a very exciting episode indeed. We did not get much information about it at the time, it was just after the war and that, of course, was a very absorbing factor. Our sympathies were very much with Lenin and the others..." (J. Nehru, *The First Sixty Years*, New York, 1965, Vol. 1, p. 57).

In October 1927 the Indian newspaper *Forward* carried an article by Jawaharlal Nehru on the foreign policy of free India. Coming out resolutely for developing India's international ties, the author arrived at a bold and important conclusion for those times. He assigned the USSR an important place among the countries with which India should develop friendly relations. "India has thus every reason to develop friendly relations with Russia," he pointed out. (*Forward*, 26 October 1927). He called for a study of the constructive Soviet methods in the spheres of education, agriculture and industrialisation. He also exposed the attempts of the British colonial authorities to depict the land of Soviets as an enemy of India. "No country is perhaps more in need of peace than Russia," he stressed, "and only fear or circumstances outside her control are likely to drive her to war... India has no quarrel with Russia, she has considerable sympathy for her, and there is much in her that she admires." Moreover, Nehru warned his compatriots against a real danger for India—to "be dragged into a war against Russia for the benefit of British imperialism".

Such a statement of Jawaharlal Nehru in the Indian press to all intents and purposes was a bold call to his compatriots to change their distorted ideas about the USSR. His was the first firm voice raised inside the leadership of the Indian National Congress in favour of a friendly attitude towards the Soviet Union.

During their stay in Europe, Jawaharlal and his father Motilal received from the USSR Society for Cultural Relations with Foreign Countries (VOKS) an invitation to visit the Soviet Union during the celebrations of the 10th anniversary of the Great October Socialist Revolution. In the beginning of November 1927 Motilal, Jawaharlal, Kamala and Krishna left Berlin for Moscow via Poland. The arrival of these eminent figures of the Indian national-liberation movement was awaited with great interest in Moscow. The *Pravda* stated on 5 November 1927: "One of the most eminent leaders of the Indian National movement, Pandit Motilal Nehru, is arriving here..." After giving a brief account of his political activity, the newspaper continued: "He will arrive in Moscow accompanied by his son Jawaharlal, the leader of the Left-wing in the National Congress."

The Nehru family arrived in Moscow on the afternoon of 8 November 1927. Jawaharlal Nehru later wrote that they were all sorry that they had not arrived a day or two earlier, and thus missed the chance of seeing the parade and procession of a million people brimming with enthusiasm. The stay of the Nehru family in Moscow was very short but extremely full. They were interested in all the aspects of Soviet life. They visited the Bolshoi Theatre. Of this Jawaharlal said enthusiastically: "The artistes danced amazingly well. Altogether from the point of view of beauty and art it was a show difficult to beat anywhere in the world. (J. Nehru, *Soviet Russia*, Bombay, 1949, p. 15). He also gave a high appraisal of a Soviet film dedicated to the Revolution. "It was a very powerful and stirring film," he pointed out. "It showed the contrast between luxury and misery in the days of the Tsar, and then the ghastly scenes of the war. The downfall of the Tsar, the Kerensky government and the fight for power between the Bolsheviks and Kerensky, ending with Lenin's victory, were shown very effectively.

The Nehrus also visited the Mausoleum of V.I. Lenin, "the greatest of all men", to whom Jawaharlal devoted later a special section in his book.

The programme of Motilal and Jawaharlal Nehru's stay in Moscow included also meeting prominent Soviet statesmen. They had talks with M.I. Kalinin, Chairman of the Central Executive Committee of the USSR (the legislative body corresponding to the present-day Presidium of the USSR Supreme Soviet), and USSR People's Commissar of Foreign Affairs G.V. Chicherin.

The general impression of the Nehru family of their Moscow visit was expressed by Jawaharlal in the following warm words: "Our stay in Moscow was too short for us to see much. But short as it was, it was enough to make us feel the fascination of this beautiful city. We came away with regret and with the desire to see again its golden domes shining in the sun, and its streets and squares full of strange people from the east and the west." The letter was published in the Lahore newspaper *Tribune,* on 13 December 1927 (vide L.V. Mitrokhin's article "Jawaharlal Nehru in Moscow in 1927", *Link,* No. 13, 1967, p. 40). He wrote about the strength and novelty of his impressions of Moscow already on the third day of his stay in the Soviet Union, in a letter dated 10 November 1927, to his elder sister Vijayalakshmi Pandit: "We are in a topsy-turvy land. All one's old values get upset and life wears a strange aspect here... the spirit of equality is rampant and pride in the revolution." (Ibid.)

As distinct from his son, Motilal Nehru did not leave any recollections about his stay in the Soviet Union. Nonetheless, testimonies of people close to him show the positive impact the trip to the USSR made on him.

"To my father all such Soviet and collectivist ideas were wholly novel," Jawaharlal Nehru explained. "His whole training had been legal and constitutional, and he could not easily get out of that framework. But he was definitely impressed by what he saw in Moscow." (J. Nehru, *An Autobiography*, Bombay, 1962, p. 165).

Being an honest and courageous fighter for his country's independence, Motilal Nehru came out many a time in the years after his visit to the USSR, it is well known, in defence of the land of Soviets and the Indian Communists from the slander and repressive actions of the colonial authorities.

For Jawaharlal Nehru the trip to the USSR was of especially deep significance. This far-sighted political figure was interested in the positive experience of the Soviet Union's development that could be utilised in India free from British rule. Summing up this trip, Jawaharlal later noted: "But we were glad we went, for even that glimpse was worthwhile. It did not, and could not, teach us much about the new Russia, but it did give us a background for our reading." (J. Nehru, *An Autobiography*, op. cit.)

On the basis of personal impressions and the literature he had read, Jawaharlal wrote in 1928 a whole series of articles about the USSR in the daily *Hamdard, Hindu* and other Indian newspapers. (All this material was collected in his book *Soviet Russia,* published in Bombay in the beginning of 1929.)

His objective approach to the problems under consideration made it possible for him to present on the whole a correct picture of the USSR, though some social processes and features of Soviet life were not fully understood by him.

Jawaharlal Nehru's book about the Soviet Union aroused tremendous interest in India. His writings on the development in the Soviet Union that were published in India led, beginning from 1928–1929, to a wide flow of letters from Indians of all ages and convictions to the VOKS and other Soviet organisations for additional material on the developments in the USSR, or for arranging permanent exchange of information between their authors and Soviet people.

The articles and books by the great son of India which shed light on the situation in the USSR constituted a powerful blow at the anti-Soviet campaign carried on for years by the British colonialists in India. For many thousands of Indians they were a true discovery of new Russia.

(*Soviet Land,* November 1967)

25

India's National-Liberation Movement and Socialism at the Start of the 20th Century

A.V. Raikov

Western Orientologists advocate a theory which says that the countries of the East should develop in their own peculiar way having nothing in common with the general laws typical of the rest of the world. This theory is very often used by those who would like to drive a wedge between the newly-liberated countries of Asia and the socialist countries. They also try to "prove" that socialist principles cannot be applied to Eastern countries. They deliberately overlook the fact that there has always been an objective basis for unity between the national-liberation movement of the East and the international working-class movement, namely, the struggle against their common enemy—imperialism. Apart from the development of capitalist relations and the emergence of an industrial proletariat, it was also this factor which significantly contributed to the spread of socialist ideas to countries struggling for their independence.

In this respect it is very instructive to refer to India's national-liberation movement since it has always had in it a radical current the representatives of which have been particularly receptive to progressive ideas coming from the West—i.e., the ideas of scientific socialism. These ideas began emerging in India because the international proletariat had been a consistent ally of the Indian people in their struggle for national liberation and because the struggle against foreign oppression in India unequivocally raised the demand for social reforms. The development of the Indian proletariat consolidated the social base the ideological expression of which was scientific socialism.

The birth of a new class in India, possessing vast potentialities, was immediately taken note of by the most far-sighted leaders of the national-liberation movement. Among them was Aurobindo Ghosh, an active member of the national-liberation movement. Back in 1894, when India had no organised working-class movement, he wrote a series of articles in the newspaper *Hindu Prakash* emphasising the role of the proletariat in society. "The proletariat, as I strove to show, is the principal key to the situation. Being lethargic, it is unable to wake up and take action but it is a great potential force. He who will be able to understand and assess this will thereby become the master of the future," he wrote.*

Several years later, Swami Vivekananda predicted that the "time will come when the *shudra* would take power". There is no doubt that by the *shudra* he meant the working masses, the proletariat of his time. What Vivekananda had in mind was that the *shudra* would exercise "undivided rule in all countries throughout the world".

It can be presumed that Aurobindo Ghosh and Vivekananda developed such ideas under the influence of Marxist literature.

Characteristically, progressive thinkers in India at that time did not only pose the question of the country's liberation. They also thought about the path of development which independent India of the future would embark upon. By the end of the 19th century and at the start of the 20th, India's political literature started rejecting the idea that the country must turn back to the past, to some "golden age" of patriarchal communes, of the pre-British period. Progressive people in India spread another idea that was rapidly winning popularity, namely, that the country must build a new society. But what should it be like? Even the most radical thinkers in India,

* All quotations appearing in this article are re-translated from Russian.

early in the 20th century, were not able to offer a definite answer to this question. One thing was clear: they did not hold the view any longer that India must take the capitalist path of development. In their works, India's radicals sharply criticised capitalism though not from a proletarian standpoint.

They rejected capitalism because it had brought India colonial enslavement, poverty and famine. More than that, after some years of emigration, many Indians came to realise that the working masses in the West were also deprived of rights and were mercilessly exploited. In her well-known "Message to the People of India", Madame Cama, an outstanding Indian revolutionary, wrote in Britain: "We do not want to copy British civilisation. No, gentlemen, we shall have our own civilisation that will be more progressive and noble. What is Morley's civilisation? (Minister for India's Affairs—AVR). The persecution of women only because they demand human rights. And what do I see throughout this country? Poverty, starvation, plunder and despotism."

In setting forth the task of carrying out democratic reforms and the social emancipation of masses, the Indian patriotic democrats came to realise that independence alone was not enough and that it meant very little just to set up an Indian government instead of the British. In his newspaper *Kesari* (9 April 1907) Tilak wrote that a mere absence of foreign government and the presence of India's own could no longer satisfy modern minds. He cited the examples of the socialist movements of Russia and Germany.

Activists of the Indian national-liberation movement sought support from the international working-class and socialist movement. In his speech at the Congress of the Second International in Amsterdam in 1904, the veteran of the Indian National Congress, Dadabhai Nauroji, said that he had come there to seek the sympathy and support of the international proletariat for oppressed India. At the Stuttgart Congress of the Second International, Madame Cama made an impassioned speech against the British colonialists. But the International was at that time controlled by opportunist leaders and, instead of rendering practical assistance to the oppressed people, it only adopted general declarations blaming the colonial authorities for abusing power. At that time, when the activists of the national-liberation movement were becoming interested in the socialist movement, the Second International, particularly, the British Socialists, should have established contacts with this movement and helped spread socialist ideas in India. The Second International, however, did not fulfil this task. Characteristically, for example, in his book *The Awakening of India* (published in 1910) the British Labour leader, R. MacDonald, did not even mention the Indian working class which had emerged on the political arena by that time.

True, when in 1910 British workers' leader, Keir Hardy, visited India he helped set up in Calcutta the Social-Democratic League—the first socialist organisation in India. The British working-class newspaper, *Labour Leader*, wrote effusively about that event: "We convey to our Indian comrades our hearty congratulations since they are the first to have raised the red banner in India. In them we see the propagandists of the great cause and we foresee the time when the banners of socialism will be raised in every city of Bengal." But after Keir Hardy's departure, the Labour Party members showed no interest in the League's activities. Not for nothing did *The Times of India* write (on 15 January 1910) that whenever the Indian workers tried to come into contact with the Labour Party, they met nothing else but ostracism on the part of MacDonald's friends.

If the reformists of the Second International did not support Indian patriots, the Russian Social Democrats, who represented the revolutionary trend in the international working-class movement, on the contrary, used every opportunity to help spread socialist ideas. In Paris, M. Pavlovich did a great deal to help Indian revolutionaries. His contacts with V. Chattopadhyaya and his friendly relationship with Madame Cama are well known. He remembered that in his flat he often discussed plans for revolutionary work with Indian, Persian and Chinese revolutionaries who were his regular guests. He also edited leaflets written by Indian revolutionary leaders. When Indians formed a circle in Paris to study sociology, history and scientific socialism, among its teachers were also Russian Social Democrats. Similarly, the Russian revolutionaries in America helped spread the ideas of socialism among Indian immigrants. The 1905 Russian Revolution deepened the interest of the leaders of the Indian national-liberation movement in social problems.

Indian patriots also showed keen interest in the first political action of the Indian proletariat during the 1905–1908 revolutionary upsurge in India arising under the influence of the 1905 Russian Revolution. Thus, in his magazine *Free Hindustan,* the Indian revolutionary, Tarknath Das, wrote that during the 1908 events in Bombay the workers showed themselves as ardent fighters for the cause of independence. On the whole, all this deepened interest in socialist ideas. It is not accidental that in 1909 the *Vedik Magazine,* brought out by Prof. Rama Deva, published one of the first essays ever written in an Indian periodical on the history of socialist doctrines. It correctly analysed Marx's basic ideas on the decisive role of the economic factor in society and of the working class as the producer of all wealth and as its rightful master. The author wrote: "We are most interested in the well-grounded prediction of Marx about the inevitable offensive of socialism in the near future."

The British colonial authorities even at that time sensed the threat, and launched an offensive against the penetration of progressive ideas.

Of course, at that time only a small number of Indians were familiar with the ideas of scientific socialism and they were not able to understand these completely. Nevertheless, the first steps in this direction had been taken.

The ideas of scientific socialism spread on a wide scale in India after the 1917 October Revolution. One should not, however, underestimate the role of those Indian patriots who were working hard for laying the ground for this process when there was no socialist state in the world and when the proletarian revolution seemed a matter of the distant future.

(*Soviet Land,* November 1966)

26

Recalling the Grim Tragedy of Amritsar

L. Mitrokhin and A. Raikov

In April 1969, on the occasion of the 50th anniversary of the gruesome massacre in Amritsar, India commemorated the death-defying martyrs of struggle against British imperialism. New books were published, newspapers carried numerical articles, telling the new generations of Indians about the monstrous brutalities committed by the colonialists. Historians have substantial documentary evidence about these events, since back in 1920, soon after the events, reports by the government and congressional commissions, and facts collected by them were made public. Hardly anything new, it seemed, could be added to these materials. Nevertheless, quite unexpectedly historians found a volume of secret documents, of which nothing had been known previously.

It was presumed that the Hunter Commission, which officially investigated the events, made public, besides the report, five volumes of evidence it had collected about the disturbances in Punjab and the shooting in Amritsar. It has been found out recently, however, that there was still another volume, the sixth.* The inscription "confidential" clearly shows that the British printed it not for the public at large and, probably, only a few copies of it. One of the copies fell into the hands of researchers only 50 years later.

The very table of contents makes clear why the colonialists did not want these documents to be known to the public. Their authors were in most cases not members of the punitive expedition like General Dyer, and not ordinary Indians, witnesses to the events, but the makers of the colonial policy. The more important documents include the official report of the Punjab Government presented to the Hunter Commission; the verbose notes of the top British officials of Punjab like Michael O'Dwyer and Thompson as well as various references, memoranda, extracts from the Punjab government's diary, materials concerning the activity of revolutionary organisations and clippings from the Indian press.

The documents throw a flood of light on the various aspects of the situation in Punjab and on the policy of the colonial government of India at the beginning of the '20s. Whether the compilers of the volume wanted it or not, everything in it ended in one event—the shooting in Jallianwala Bagh Square. Thus it reveals the real nature of the tragic events of 13 April 1919, underlining the one circumstance, which often escaped the attention of researchers: the events in Amritsar had very definite connection with the October Revolution in Russia.

The documents of the sixth volume show, in part, the British authorities' reaction to the upsurge of the liberation movement in India under the influence of the Proletarian Revolution in Russia as well as the colonialists' attitude to the events in Russia.

This theme found in the secret documents a contradictory reflection. On the one hand, an attempt was made to show that India was threatened by the "Bolshevik invasion". In confirmation absurd opinions were cited to allege that Amritsar was the centre of activities of the "Bolshevik agents". Since this allegation was not confirmed by any concrete facts, the Punjab government tried to find new "arguments" of the following type: "Amritsar, it may be added, is also the rendezvous of the Central Asian merchants who, as has already been pointed out, are the possible agents of the Bolsheviks."

In the government statement even the Satyagraha movement headed by Gandhi was called a "Conspiracy originated or supported from outside". This absurd assertion served only as another pretext for pointing at the "Bolshevik intrigues".

From the documents of the sixth volume of the Hunter Commission one can see quite an obvious fear of penetration into India of the Bolshevik ideas, which could serve as an example for the Indians. This fear, as a matter of fact, determined much in the policy of the colonialists.

The very same Thompson admitted in his testimony that, besides the direct causes of disturbances in Punjab in 1919 (protest against the Rowlatt's Act, rising prices, increasing taxation, the Moslems' discontent with the British policy in Turkey, etc.), a great anxiety was aroused by "other causes".

"What about the Bolshevik movement?" asked Hunter. "Yes", Thompson answered.

Finally, Thompson was asked a question which summed up his evidence in a definite way "Suppose a soil saturated with the doctrine of passive resistance would be very fruitful for the growth of the Bolshevik ideas?". "I think so, my lord", Thompson replied, "After all they both encourage defiance of law and existing institutions".

Almost the same views were expressed in the Hunter Commission by O'Dwyer. Before the October Revolution he visited Russia and on that ground, regarding himself as an expert in the "Russian question", developed the idea that Leo Tolstoy was the "forerunner of Bolshevism". And since Gandhi's doctrine, O'Dwyer believed was "almost an exact parallel to the Tolstoy's doctrine", it could lead to the same results as in Russia. What results did O'Dwyer consider most undesirable and dangerous for the British? "Tolstoy's doctrine", he said, "was making headway when I was in Russia and I discussed it with many members of Russian intelligentsia who were rushing at it at the time as a means to curb the powers of autocracy. I said to them: 'You don't know what forces you are unleashing'." He clearly had in view a people's revolution. Not understanding at all either the essence of the Revolution in Russia, or the sources of Bolshevism, O'Dwyer thought that he was right in sounding a warning. Without repeating before the Commission fabrications of the bourgeois press about the October Revolution, he was frank to the utmost: most of all what he feared in any revolution was that "the masses become masters of the situation".

The fear that a similar thing might happen in India explained the nervous attention with which the colonial government regarded any inspiration derived by the Indians from the ideas of the Great October Revolution. As of an important event, the Hunter Commission was informed of the arrival of a group of Indian revolutionaries in Moscow. The government report mentioned Bolshevik propaganda conducted by Indian revolutionaries who had ties with the Russian Bolsheviks.

A number of secret documents give an idea of the anxiety which the Soviet government's foreign policy created in the minds of India's rulers, the policy aimed at giving aid to the people fighting for independence. The book contains the texts of the intercepted radiograms sent from Tashkent to Moscow," telling of the receipt of letters from Kabul addressed to the Soviet government. The British were especially alarmed at the statement made by the king of Afghanistan that "Russia, by raising the standard of Bolshevism, had earned the gratitude of the whole world" as well as at the Afghanistan's Foreign Minister's statement to establish friendly relations with Soviet Russia.

The authorities, no doubt, drew an analogy between Afghanistan's friendly attitude to the Soviet state and the possibility of similar sentiments in Punjab. This is clear also from an extract quoted from an article in the newspaper *Siyasat* of 6 April 1919. Its writer showed much sympathy with the overthrow of Tsarism in Russia and welcomed the Bolsheviks' coming to power. The remark in the article that "the great powers of Europe regard the Bolsheviks' government with a feeling of extreme hatred and anxiety" fully applied to the colonial authorities of Punjab and the whole of India.

Whatever representatives of the colonial authorities might mean by giving account of these data, one thing is certain: they felt the natural connection between the proletarian revolution in Russia and the liberation movement in India and other countries of the East. The Punjab Government's attitude to the people's actions was determined by the fear that in India, too, the people might become "masters of the situation". And although in Punjab, just as in the whole of India, the movement remained, on the whole, non-violent, the authorities feared that it could turn violent and serve as a basis for the spread of the Bolshevik ideas.

A great alarm was caused by the attitude of the working-class. Thompson admitted before the commission that the growing strike movement, especially in the railways, alarmed the government very much. In its statement to the commission the government pointed out that the working-class problem "has started developing in India". And it knew very well that in the working class the Bolshevik ideas spread most quickly.

The documents included in the sixth "confidential" volume of the Hunter Commission show that, seized with panic, the British authorities in Punjab adopted early in April important decisions. On 10 April the governor made an obviously threatening statement in his public speech: "This movement, unless promptly checked, will bring about disorder and bloodshed." But it could be promptly checked only by force of arms. A sinister plan was worked out in this connection. The city chosen to carry it through was Amritsar. The job was handed over to General Dyer, who understood the scheme of the authorities killing and wounding 2,000 participants of the meeting in Jallianwala Bagh. The documents of the secret volume of the Hunter Commission show that the bloody reprisal was planned as an intimidating measure not only for Amritsar but also for the whole of India.

The subsequent events showed that neither that massacre, nor other brutal measures helped the British to suppress the Indian people's will to struggle.

(*Soviet Land*, April 1967)

27

Lenin and India's Liberation Movement after the October Revolution

E. Komarov

Led by Lenin, Soviet Russia was the first state in history which, despite the tremendous difficulties involved in the building of a new social system and in the repulsing of the aggression of its enemies, found the strength and had the determination to render every possible support to the people of the East in their struggle against imperialist oppression. As far back as July 1917, on the eve of the victorious October Revolution, Lenin wrote: "The Russian revolution, which as early as 1905 led to revolutions in Turkey, Persia and China, would have placed the German and the British imperialists in a very difficult position if it had begun to establish a truly revolutionary alliance of the workers and peasants of the colonies and semi-colonies against the despots, against the khans, for expulsion of Germans from Turkey, the British from Turkey, Persia, India, Egypt, etc."

Heading the Soviet state and laying the foundations of its policy of support to the oppressed people, Lenin took a lively interest in the progress of the national-liberation struggle in India that was reaching a new, higher stage in those years. Lenin pointed out this fact in his message to India in 1920. He spoke of the "awakening of the Indian workers and peasants" and greeted the "progressive Indians, who were waging a heroic fight for freedom". He made a special mention of the need for unity between Hindus and Moslems for the success of the liberation struggle. His message ended with the words: "Long Live a Free Asia!" In 1921, Lenin noted the outstanding role of India among the countries whose people were struggling for national liberation : "British India is at the head of these countries, and there revolution is maturing in proportion, on the one hand, to the growth of the industrial and railway proletariat, and, on the other, to the increase in the brutal terrorism of the British, who with ever greater frequency resort to massacres (Amritsar), public floggings, etc."

It must be pointed out that by far not all were able to assess correctly the specific features of the socio-political development in India. This led to a distorted sectarian assessment of the course of the national liberation struggle in India and of the role of its leaders, particularly Mahatma Gandhi. As has become known now, Lenin was against such an assessment. There were particularly sharp differences between him and M.N. Roy over the attitude to Gandhi. Roy describes in his reminiscences that, in Lenin's view, by organising and leading the mass anti-imperialist struggle Gandhi was playing a revolutionary role. Arguing with Roy at a discussion that took place in the commission on the national and colonial questions of the Second Congress of the Comintern in 1921, Lenin, according to the record of the proceedings, said: "We in Russia supported the liberal-liberation movement in the name of coming out against Tsarism. The Indian Communists must support the bourgeois-democratic movement without merging with it."

Lenin's policy was aimed at the setting up of a united front of all anti-imperialist and anti-feudal forces in the countries oppressed by imperialism, at bringing about an alliance of the national-liberation movement with the international working-class movement, with Soviet Russia—the world's first socialist country.

The Indians who had met Lenin, like everyone else who had occasion to work with him, noted his exceptional attentiveness and modesty. M.N. Roy describes his meetings with Lenin as follows: "Lenin's attitude was highly benevolent and tolerant... That was, perhaps, the most valuable thing I had met in my life till then. I had a rare and happy chance of meeting a great man who treated me as an equal, showing his greatness, in this way." (Roy was referring to the Second Comintern Congress).

Although the situation in Soviet Russia was very tense and although Lenin was tremendously busy, he not only strove to know as much as possible about India (which is evident from the lists of books he ordered) but he also wanted that knowledge about India be spread throughout Soviet Russia. Recommending Abani Mukerji's article, Lenin wrote to the editor of the *Pravda*:

"Please read this. We ought... to publish more material by Indian comrades so as to encourage them and collect more information on India and its revolutionary movement."

In the months immediately following the victory of the October Revolution, Lenin received the Secretary of the Academy of Sciences, a well-known Indologist S.F. Oldenburg, whom he had known in his younger days. V. Bonch-Bruyevich, who was present at the meeting, records what Lenin told Oldenburg:

"Take your subject... it seems to be far removed from us, yet it is near to us... Go to the masses, to the workers and tell them about the history of India, about the ages of the sufferings of those unfortunate multi-million masses, enslaved by the English, and you will see how the masses of our proletariat will respond. And you yourself will be inspired to new quests, to new research, to new work of great scientific importance."

(*Soviet Land*, September 1972)

28

Early Contacts Between India and Russia

P.M. Kemp

Indo-Russian contact is first of all a geographic fact. The two countries are contiguous at least at one point on the border line. Naturally, human intercourse which defies all barriers and obstacles and always strives forth is bound to exist between two such lands from times immemorial.

When the first human contact between the two countries was established is not yet ascertained. Perhaps it is difficult to do so. But to start with it can be said with a certain amount of assurance that the first Russians to visit India were brought here as slaves.

For many centuries the borders of Russian territories were raided by successive neighbours for captives, and in early times Slav tribesmen, like others, under stress of famine sold themselves, their children and other people's children into bondage. In old times the Volga towns of Itil and Bulgar and later Kazan supplied the oriental slave market. Throughout the Arab East Russian slaves, valued for their hardiness, were dispersed far afield. They formed the bodyguard of a Spanish Caliph in the West and found their place in the Court of the Great Moghul in the East, where several travellers from Western Europe met Russians in the 16th–17th century. It has been estimated that in the early 16th century the Kazan Tatars captured up to 200,000 Russians whom they traded to

Baghdad, Bukhara and other markets which in the Muslim period supplied foreign slaves for the Indian court and nobility.

Ideas about Russia in Medieval India

Indian medieval literature acquired a set of stereotyped ideas about Russia from the writings of the Arab geographers who had given detailed accounts of the people in the Volga basin, from the penetration of a few Russian commodities via the ancient trade routes from that region, and from the living contacts with slaves.

The Russians were supposed to be very rough and warlike—the bravest people in the world according to Awfi. They were supposed to share many of the qualities that appealed to the medieval feudal ideal, but their women, though beautiful, were "blocks of ice". Their noteworthy products were superior mail and remarkable swords,* hunting hawks and dogs and later horses. Fine Russian flax, when it could be got, was reserved by royal decree for use as khalats bestowed by the king.

The wide ramifications of the Alexander legend in literature supplied other references to Russia, just as in its Byzantine and Slavonic versions the Alexander saga told the Russian reader about the marvels of India. The romance of Nizam's Russian princess lent her features to the Indian picture of Catherine II in the 18th century and bequeathed to Urdu literature the Russian heroine of Fazana Azad in the period of Anglo-Russian imperialist rivalry when Indian leaders of 1857 had looked hopefully to the Russian government for support.

Amir Khusru celebrated the heroism of Russian in the army of Ghazi Malik when Khusru Khan was defeated in 1320 and the Muslim kingdom of Delhi restored. These brave Russians were probably slave soldiers in the King's army. In that case they had perhaps originally been uprooted from their homeland as a result of Mongol incursions into Russia.

* The Russians originally exported swords from the famous armourers of the Rhine but later manufactured their own for trade to the East.

Possibly they were converts to Islam, as the poet suggests, but they may have fought enthusiastically because they were under the impression that they faced an old enemy of their own.

A legend circulated in Central Asia that the Russians had embraced Islam in the time of Prince Vladimir of Kiev. They were said to have retained some Pagan habits, like eating pork. This legend was incorporated by Awfi along with all the most entertaining material about the Russian Slav regions available in older writers. His book, completed on Indian soil, remained a great authority on Indo-Persian polymathic literature for many generations. When in the late 18th century French and English penetration forced the need for more up-to-date information about Europe, an Indian writer for the King still had to clear up a doubt as to whether the Russians were Muslim, Christian or Pagan.

Living Contacts of Traders Abroad

Medieval polite literature, however, is nowhere a true measure of the practical knowledge current in other spheres. There were other circles in India who knew much more about Russia through direct contact than what they got from contemporary books.

These were first and foremost those enterprising Indian merchants who ramified their business connections far and wide through the Middle East, in Central Asia and to China, and in the course of time had established large stable agencies in all the main trading centres lying along all the routes between Northern India and the limits of Russian influence.

Direct contact between Indian and Russian traders in the old towns of the Volga basin went back to the early 10th century (when Ibn Fadlan recorded their presence in the Khazar capital) and probably much earlier. Later, Russians and Indians did business together in Bukhara and other Central Asian markets. Jenkinson, travelling under the protection of the Moscow government in search of an overland route to India, saw merchants there "from the Ganges" and from Bengal, from whom the Russians bought the precious indigo, that was re-exported by Germans in the West. While Indian merchants and bankers flourished in all the Persian centres from Hornmuz to the Caspian, Russians at one time ran their own camel caravans between Tabriz and Baghdad and traded down to the Persian Gulf, whence, among other things, they brought the seed pearls lavishly used in old Russian costume and head dresses, and known to them by the trade name of "kedgeree".

The written travelogues of one of these Russian merchants in the 17th century have survived. He described in particular the condition and habits of Indians in various places on the way, particularly the large colony at Isphahan, and gave details of the route from Hormuz by land to Lahore and Delhi. This road was used particularly by horse dealers of various nationalities including Russians, who joined together for the enterprise.

There can be no doubt, therefore, that individual Russians must have made the journey to India both via Persia and Bukhara. This is confirmed by the statement of a Russian ambassador in Central Asia. In 1620 he chanced to meet one of them who had spent several years in India.

By the end of the century Russians had direct contact with Kabul and regular caravans linked up Kabul, Samarkand and Bukhara with Astrakhan and Tobolsk. Other individuals travelled along with companies of Bukharian traders and made difficult and dangerous journeys through Afghanistan, Badakhshan, Tibet and Eastern Turkestan, where merchants of many nations went in search of rare drugs, musk, saffron, rhubarb and precious stones.

The unsettled conditions of the intervening Kazak steppes and the hostility of the Khanates frequently closed the trade routes, but these living contacts must have continued for centuries in spite of interruptions.

After the fall of Constantinople the only routes open to travellers from the West, either to China or India, lay through Russian territory. Permission to traverse their country and to buy oriental goods there was a regular matter of negotiation in Russian diplomatic relations with other countries. The Russians were for long the experts and intermediaries for Indian trade. The English chartered company set up for Russian trade in the 16th century— the so-called Muscovy or Russian Company—till the end of its existence in the second half of the 18th century remained the weak rival of the East India Company and still claimed, in theory, exclusive monopolies in Indian and Persian wares.

Russian Information about India

Hence in the Middle Ages the scanty knowledge about India that circulated in Russia tended to be more realistic than the rumours and romances of geographers in Western Europe. With the expansion of the Mongol hordes westward it may be said that for the first time Russian and Indian history came to intersect. The Russian chronicles include a contemporary history of Timur, for instance, including his campaigns in India.

Even much earlier, Russian folk epic and oral tradition seemed to reflect tenuous but real contact with India and Indian products. A very popular folk song current for many centuries is a story about India. Here India was what the land of Cokayn represented in the West, for the well-to-do a longed-for eldorado for adventurers, for the hungry peasant a dream of never ending food, drink and comfort for all.

This folk song went on to say that from this far-off land of marvels a fabulously rich, charming young stranger arrived at the Court of the Great Prince of Kiev and was hospitably received. To settle a wager with the Russian champions, Russian envoys were sent to India and returned with a report that not all the wealth of Kiev would suffice to buy the paper and ink necessary for making an inventory of the riches of his home.

At the end of the story the Great Prince granted the Indian hero perpetual rights to trade in his realms free of all dues, just as in the later middle ages Indian merchants in Russia enjoyed special privileges and duty free trade.

There are enough hints in the various details of the epic that the India intended was a real if little known country with which certain specific peculiarities were associated, some borrowed from literary works and some perhaps from popular information.

If this imaginary hero represented in any sense a popular idea about Indian character, it should be noted that he is a very pleasing and amusing figure in folk epic, in contrast to the way in which popular bards usually depicted their pagan and Muslim neighbours as ferocious villains and Ogres. In one version of the story the most popular of all the Russian folk epic heroes paternally takes the young Indian under his wing in case his innocence is exploited. In another the young man's horse claims to be the brother of the horses of the best Russian champions.

Other stories of literary origin circulated about India in the early medieval period, and one of the popular saints of the Russian Church calendar was supposed to be a pious Indian King, whose biography naturally conveyed a favourable popular impression of that country.

The First Russian Friend of India

The travels of Afanasii Nikitin (15th century), the first European to visit and write about India at first hand since the days of Alexander, are, of course, well-known to historians. The work has been quoted at length for instance in Sewell's history of Vijiyanagar. He took it unfortunately from a faulty English translation dated 1857. Minaev, the well-known specialist in Buddhism, who himself wrote a highly interesting travel book about India in the 19th century, established the authenticity of Nikitin's record and first pointed out how it supplemented Ferishta's material for the period. For other reasons Nikitin's book in modern times gained a recognised place in medieval Russian literature. Recently a fine definitive edition in the facsimiles of original MSS has been published by the Russian Academy of Science. A number of popular modern editions of it are available for general readers and schools.

Nikitin's book is partly a very matter-of-fact record and partly a rather intimate journal of his personal affairs and feelings. It contains none of the tales of marvels that Western books of the period circulated about India. Perhaps his intention was to give a written report to the patrons or officials who may, in the first instance, have encouraged his adventure—but he died on the way back to his home and the precious manuscript was taken by a government clerk to Moscow and there copied and carefully preserved. Unwittingly Nikitin left a remarkably human document that brings down the centuries a vivid picture of his age and his own emotional reactions.

The travellers from Western Europe who later came to India in their own ships, laden with attractive luxuries, mostly brought letters from their respective monarchs and presented themselves at Court. Nikitin did not mix in such high circles. He was a small man, and arrived in India after being robbed of his merchandise. At times, one gathers, he must have been up against great difficulties, and pondered sorrowfully whether he would ever again see his own land. Consequently he saw India from a very different angle. He mixed with people of a lower class, made friends with them, visited their homes and saw their family life from close quarters. With Hindu friends he went to local fairs, entered into local trade and adapted himself to their customs.

Nikitin was obliged to travel disguised as a foreign Muslim. He was afraid of being discovered and persecuted by Muslim officials. Even disguised, he was only a poor trader without protection and suffered at their hands on several occasions. But to the non-Muslims, the "Hindustanis", he revealed that he was really "Afanasi, the Russian". Alone in a strange country and not very fortunate, it must have meant much to be able to talk freely, probably share grievances against the administration, and say what you felt about religion.

The ruling class in India he represented as foreign Muslim conquerors, who lived in great splendour, supported by a powerful army and bureaucracy, sharply cut off from the masses of "black" Indians. He has several comments to make on the extreme poverty and frugality of all classes. These observations may be read as a comment on the limited scope of commerce, since his final verdict was that Russian goods would not find a market in India. The poor and the middling could not buy, local goods were too cheap, and the rich were amply provided with luxuries by cheap labour. The cheapness of human life including the price of female slaves and prostitutes struck him forcibly.

If Nikitin's standard of comparison were the conditions of feudal serfs and peasantry in Russia and the Middle East of the 15th century, these passages are all the more significant.

Near the end of his book Nikitin seems to have summed up the lessons of his experiences in a rather obscure passage which he discreetly put in the Turkish dialect, lingua franca of traders in Central Asia. It expresses both his homesickness and his view of life generally.

"May God preserve the Russian land! God save her! There is no country in the world like her, though the Russian nobles be unjust (not wealthy). May the Russian land be well ordered and justice (righteousness) be there; you have little truth (justice)".

Whether he meant that Russia was the best place to live in, despite the absence of very great wealth even in the upper classes, or whether he meant that in spite of the oppressions of the nobility it was still home, it is clear that the main idea expressed is the cry for "justice", "right", "order". He had seen and suffered a vastly more complete autocracy, a thorough monopoly control of wealth and power and even of trade and industry, backed by a powerfully organised administration, the like of which did not exist in all Europe.

The lesson seems to be that it is after all "justice" that matters and that in his own country there is also much amiss. If this interpretation is anywhere near correct, then Nikitin's India was seen through the eyes of a common man who vaguely anticipated the democratic tendencies that would later arise in the cities of Europe.

In contrast, the Portuguese and English adventurers to India were from the outset obsessed with the riches of India. They were mainly concerned with how they might extract hidden treasure, plunder the plunderer and establish their own supremacy as had been done in South America.

Mahmud Gavan, then at the height of his power, appears in Nikitin's story as a sort of evil genius—the prime example of tyranny, greed, ostentation and bigotry. Ferishta made him a hero and a mild patron of learning. Nikitin shows him perverting elementary justice, grabbing war plunder for his exclusive use and waging unprovoked war for the purpose of capturing hordes of Hindus, not only war prisoners, but women and children as well, to be sold as slaves.

In the context of his other remarks, Nikitin's description of this grand slave raid suggests that he felt compassion for the slaves and was perhaps reminded of the similar slave raids into Russian territory. The long struggle of Russia against Tatar invaders was a very recent and bitter memory. It may have had something to do with Nikitin's sympathy for the "Hindustanis", oppressed by Muslim conquerors from abroad. The religious toleration and freedom for traders which he noted under Hindu rule in Vijiyanagar, no doubt helped to determine his political sympathies.

He writes with unexpected tolerance of Hindu religious and social customs. In spite of the deep-rooted superstition of his age, he thought he detected points in common with Hindus. Like Russians, for instance, they prayed towards the East not to Mecca. In their "83 faiths" or castes he saw a common unity and discovered that all worshipped one supreme deity. As though travel had taught him that the outward forms of orthodoxy were not everything; he exclaims, "And the true faith God knows and true faith is to call upon his name in every place".

And again he hid this dangerous heretical thought in a language which would not be understood by the monkish clerks who might read his manuscript.

Minaev thought that Nikitin was influenced by popular trends in Hindu mysticism. Be that as it may, in an age when Europe took for granted that Muslims and Christians should persecute one another and that Church and State should deal ruthlessly with different sects and heresies, Nikitin's remark has a humanistic touch.

Babur's Embassy to Russia

In 1532–33 an Indian, Hodja Hussein, arrived at Moscow with presents from Babur, the Padishah of India, and a letter requesting diplomatic alliance and trade relations. The ambassador was well-received, but the Russians, not being sure whether Babur was the real king or merely a feudatory prince, were non-commital in their reply. The original entries about this event and a translation of the letter were preserved in Russian foreign archives, but so far no reference to such an embassy has been traced in Indian contemporary sources. Babur had died before his envoy reached Moscow. While Babur with his orientation still that of Central Asia must have noted the growing influence of Moscow and the possible importance of Russian contact with Central Asian affairs, his successors, firmly established in India, would have had less reason to be interested. Neither side attempted to follow up the matter.

Indian Colony in Russia

Once the way was clear Indian merchants crossed the Russian border, and in the 16th–17th century they reached Kazan and Moscow. When Russian rule was extended to the Caspian a flourishing colony of Punjabi merchants became firmly established at Astrakhan round about 1615/16. Russian trade statutes of the 17th century made regular provisions specifically for the regulation of Indian merchants' activities and the sale of Indian wares.

In 1645 an Indian merchant visited Moscow and as a result of his favourable report on the government's attitude and trade facilities 25 more Indians moved from Persia to Astrakhan.

After representations had been made by the spokesman of the Indians to the Foreign Chancellery two or three years later, a special decree was issued for their protection and encouragement of their trade. The Governor of Astrakhan was instructed "to hold the Indian merchants in favour and protection above other foreigners".

Like similar colonies in Persia, that at Astrakhan was composed of several Hindu family concerns of separate communities. They were bankers and money lenders as well as traders. Some were extremely wealthy. At Astrakhan they dealt little in specifically Indian goods, except precious stones, but were in the wholesale trade in Persian goods. In the final analysis they were perhaps more concerned with money speculation than trade. This tendency was inevitably encouraged by Russian commercial policy, for although the Indians enjoyed special privileges, their enterprise was restricted by statute regulating commerce generally. Hence new arrivals from India brought with them a small capital in goods or money to invest for parasitic growth in a backward economy. For instance they supplied goods to pedlars on credit to traffic in neighbouring Tatar or Kalmyk settlements and in the 18th century advanced loans to local industrialists, but never acquired land themselves or risked financing industries of their own.

Not that they were without a spirit of enterprise. In the early 18th century they unsuccessfully petitioned for facilities to operate through the port of Archangel and to open up a trade route to China through Northern Siberia.

From contemporary Russian documents we can trace a little of the activities of Athmaram who presented the petition. He was the Pradhan of the most influential of the Astrakhan panchayats and often represented the interests of the community as a whole. Among other details we have some account of his personal interviews with Peter the Great who consulted him on the possibilities of commercial contacts with India and generally on the development of Astrakhan trade and industry. He died shortly after this proposal to explore wider international markets.

The Indians and the Academy of Science

I think that he was probably the same person who performed another role in cultural contact between Russia and India. He or perhaps another Pradhan—on a visit to Petersburg on official business, was eagerly commandeered by the German orientalist employed by the young Academy of Science, and had to stay with him for some weeks to give him lessons in Sanskrit. This contact provided the earliest first hand information on Indian languages and scripts (including Urdu and Punjabi) to be published in Russia, a piece of work which for those days even from an international standpoint was a valuable contribution to knowledge. However, the German scholar and the Indian merchant had to converse in Russian, and this led to some confusion in the details, the German mistaking some of the Indian's Russian for Indian words.*

It was also from the Astrakhan colony that the well-known scientist Pallas later collected Sanskrit and Punjabi vocabularies for the great comparative dictionary brought out by the Russian Academy. For this purpose he visited Astrakhan and left a full and most interesting account of the life and customs of the Indian colony illustrated by sketches.

Indian Life at Astrakhan

The Indians were organised in several separate "families" or communities. Probably several generations sent newcomers direct from India to carry on this branch of a family business. Whether the "families" or companies" were themselves divided by caste or not, the colony as a whole shared ceremonies but separate "families" did not interdine. There were separate panchayats which at times disputed with one another and sought separate representation to the Russian authorities, but as a general rule the whole colony was jointly represented

* For instance the Professor thought that the Indian's tribe or nation called themselves the "Torgoit". Evidently in answer to some question as to who his people were, the man had replied that they engaged in trade (Russian "Torguyut") meaning to say that he was of a merchant caste.

for dealings with the outside world. They kept themselves very much to themselves, not even joining the local guild of foreign merchants, and strictly adhered to their own social and religious customs in all respects except dress.

They were known generally as Multanis. The main body of them seem really to have come from Multan itself and others were from various places in Punjab and Sind. They belonged to Vaishnavite sects, contributed substantially to the Nathwara shrine and practised Krishna cults in their *sarai* where they had a temple or apartment equipped with images, ritual stones, etc. brought from India.

There is a contemporary account of a *Vairagi* or *Sanyasi* burial and Hindu cremations were still a curiosity to be seen at Astrakhan down to the middle of the 19th century. A permanent Brahmin and *chelas* were maintained in the *sarai*. Special decrees in the 17th century secured their freedom of worship and recognised their customary law and the rulings of their panchayats on matters affecting the internal life of their community. From all accounts they lived very peaceably and were regarded as very inoffensive hospitable people, though they did not mix socially with their neighbours. They lived their own Indian way of life in the stone *sarai* that served both for residence and business premises. They celebrated festivals like Diwali publicly, setting tables of fruits and melons in front of their houses for all comers.

Urchins of Astrakhan teased these strict vegetarians by threatening to slaughter crows or fish in their presence unless redeemed by a price.

Although never more than l/10th of the foreign merchant population, the Indians were an important factor in Astrakhan for some time. They had their own shipping on the Caspian and extensive business connections and credit arrangements in Persia and India. A 17th century French traveller described them as follows:

> *Those who without doubt contribute most to the flourishing condition of this city (Astrakhan) are the Indians or Banians—*

*idolators like the Kalmykes whose daughters they marry because they cannot ally themselves either with Cristians nor with the Mohammedans of the country; these people being very industrious and holding correspondence in almost all the ports of the Caspian Sea there are few sorts of merchandize that do not pass through their hands. So that they have likewise their quarter in one of the suburbs of the city to themselves where they enjoy the exercise of their false religion with all manner of freedom.**

Russia's Reputation for Generosity

The writer, a Jesuit, considered that this tolerance on the part of the Russians was very reprehensible. But as a matter of fact Russia gained a great reputation for friendliness as far as Indians were concerned. A number of visitors to Astrakhan including Englishmen noted that the Indians gratefully contrasted the liberalism of the Russians with the conditions in neighbouring Muslim countries. This belief spread to India itself. Burnes and other travellers in Northern India in the first half of the 19th century found that Russia enjoyed a great reputation among business communities and among those who had occasion to contact Russian caravan trade in the north. In earlier times toleration was a deliberate policy—within limits—to attract oriental trade and only in the later phases of Czarist imperialism became identified everywhere with extreme racial chauvinism. It was particularly so in the case of Muslim minorities, who were persecuted.

Indian Workers in Russia

The Astrakhan Indians practised debt slavery, an institution in those days not confined to them, and preyed particularly

---

* The merchants did not bring their families to Astrakhan but sometimes took temporary wives, either voluntary or given to them by insolvent debtors. It was alleged that a suburb of the city took its name from the mixed offspring of these unions who lived there. Occasionally an Indian left the community, married and settled down for good and merged with the local population.

on the backward Kalmyks in the neighbourhood. They also brought with them craftsmen as debtors or servants. Several requests from the Moscow government are on record asking for skilled weavers and masons to be sent to the capital. There are other references to the presence of Indian masons and joiners in the Caspian region. Little can be known about the fate of these people except that they sometimes managed to leave their masters and took employment in local industries.

Pilgrims and Priests

Besides the Brahmins in the *sarai, sanyasis* and pilgrims direct from India frequently found their way there. The eternal fires on the Aspheron peninsula had long been a place of Indian pilgrimage before Baku was taken over by the Russians. There was a permanent establishment of ascetics and the last of the devotees did not leave until after the middle of the 19th century.

On the Eastern side religious mendicants from as far away as Madras, wandering via Kashmir and Tibet into Siberia, came into touch with Russians in the 18th–19th century. Hindu merchants frequenting Central Asian centres also visited new Russian towns established along the expanding frontier of Russian influence. Some of this contact was more than casual because individual anecdotes about such encounters show that the Indians in question frequently spoke fluent Russian.

Russian caravan trade eastwards, which increased in the late 18th century and the first decades of the 19th century, was no doubt responsible for a number of Slavonic loan words in Kashmiri, the most obvious, of course, being samovar. In the same period Kashmiri shawl and fur merchants opened agencies in the Russian capital, and regular consignments were bought by Kashmiris on annual journeys to Russia.

For several centuries quite a lot of information about Russia must have circulated in Northern India. The British as they penetrated northwards were able to make use of informants with Russian connections to watch Russian activities in Asia. One of these agents in the 18th century, a Muslim merchant, supplied the East India Company with a highly interesting account of his travels through Central Asia and the Kazak steppes to Tobolsk, eventually reaching Petersburg and the Baltic. He claimed to have been received by the Empress. His account reads with some semblance of truth and it is possible that he did not report everything that passed at the interview. He said the Empress made much of him and entertained lavishly.

Russian Missions to India

Beginning in the early 17th century several attempts were made by the Russian government to send an embassy to India. Besides trade objectives the envoys were sometimes instructed to recruit skilled Indian craftsmen for work in Russia. For a long period ambassadors travelling in Persia and Central Asia had orders to collect whatever information they could about India and to discuss such matters with any Indian diplomats whom they might be able to meet abroad. Specific instructions were given to obtain details of routes to India.

However, no accredited representative of the Russian government actually reached India until 1676/7. He was turned back by the Governor of Kabul without being permitted to present his credentials to Aurangzeb on the alleged ground that as no embassy had come from Russia for generations, and that Russia was too remote to have mutual interests or cause for dispute, there was no need for such diplomatic connections. The envoy's report of his difficulties with the Governor of Kabul and his story of the intrigues of a man who had deserted from Russian service and taken employment under the King, are quite interesting.

A few years later a merchant, without any diplomatic commission, was entrusted with a substantial sum of money by the Russian government for the purchase of Indian goods. He arrived at Surat by sea in 1690. He was well received in Delhi and given a royal warrant to trade and travel freely. Unfortunately this man died on his way back to Russia, and the official records relating to his mission are fragmentary.

He stayed for about five years in India and visited Delhi and various trading centres, and also toured villages in search of suitable merchandise.

A Tribute to Indian Hospitality

The next Russian account of an Indian journey is very different. It is that of a non-commissioned officer who was captured by frontier tribesmen, sold to Bukhara from where he escaped to Kashmir. Subsequently he made his way to Calcutta via Delhi.

His travel book is neither particularly well written nor well informed. But the section dealing with his experience in Kashmir is of interest because of some first-hand accounts of that region, which are very rare. Above all it has a certain human interest. The writer was an unfortunate wanderer, of no particular standing, travelling completely unprotected and resourceless over thousands of miles and through countries devastated by wars. If he lacked the writers' gift to describe all that he must have seen, he at least remembered to record his gratitude to the people who helped him on his lonely way—fellow travellers along the road, an Indian doctor who nursed him in his own home without charge, strangers who gave him hospitality and clean clothes, passersby in the streets of Delhi who spontaneously offered to help him when he seemed at a loss, a gentleman who straightway invited him to dine and spent the night talking about Russia.

Once on Indian soil he has not a single adventure to relate of being robbed or molested. The moment he entered British India, however, he was arrested as a suspicious-looking vagabond and had to resort to a little bribery and a fiction about high connections in Russia to satisfy the English collector.

Throughout this long and hard journey on foot and by *ekka* and often enough alone, he had many such experiences and the incidents stuck in his memory.

So, although this simple fellow tells us little of scientific interest about India, his experiences as a poor traveller are a striking contrast to all the contemporary accounts by

Englishmen, full of dacoits and treacherous and hostile Hindus on the one hand and the glamour of riches on the other.

Our traveller naively tells us that when at long last he reached Calcutta he had no thought but joy to find a Greek church to remind him of home and eagerness to find a ship to take him to Europe. He tells us nothing about Calcutta except to contrast the ostentatious grandeur of the European town with the poverty-stricken hovels of Indians on the outskirts. We are left with the impression that it was that India he remembered with sympathy and friendship.

A Feudal Nobleman's View

Not long after another Russian travel book appeared which covered some of the same territory. This time it is a wealthy Georgian businessman aristocrat from Russia who toured in comfort touching Madras, Calcutta, Delhi, Srinagar, Lahore etc. His personal contacts in the cities illustrate how closely the Armenian and Georgian business communities in India had kept in touch with their relatives in the Caucasus. The ostensible object of this journey was to present a village in the Caucasus to a Georgian settled at Madras in recognition of his financial aid to the last Georgian monarch. The writer of the book like other upper class Georgians welcomed the recent annexation of his country by Russia and entered Russian service, but entertained romantic notions of chivalry of a feudal age and the glamour associated with old struggles for national independence in his native mountains. Hence in India he took pleasure in describing particularly instances of heroic fighting where Indian towns in the north had resisted British occupation. He travelled freely outside British India and his anecdotes are sometimes interesting; we get an idea of the reaction of business communities to the changes brought about by the conquest of Bengal.

Herasim Lebediev

The next Russian traveller to be noted, however, was altogether an exceptional character. For the first time we see

India through the eyes of a man of scholarship and artistic tastes, who was neither a politician nor a businessman.

In the late 18th century Herasim Lebediev, an obscure Russian musician, the son of a poor village priest, settled in Calcutta and spent over 10 years in the study of Indian languages, literature and philosophy.

Poverty had cut short Lebediev's education in his youth. It was under Bengali masters that he was first able to take up systematically such higher studies as mathematics and philosophy. In order to do so, he tells us, he was first obliged to apply himself to the grammar of his own language again. His intellectual ideas therefore matured under Indian influence and he did not approach this new environment with the ready-made theories and prejudices either of the learned world or of the officials.

He found his teachers and intimate friends from among Bengali Brahmin intellectuals. He faithfully reflected their ideological trends in the troubled period of the Permanent Settlement.

The Brahmin intellectual and religious circles were then regarded by the British as perhaps their most dangerous enemies, who would never co-operate with the new rulers, scorned to mix with them socially and obstinately refused to impart information on any subject. Lebediev's intimate and friendly relations in such circles were exceptional for any European at that time.

But more—he himself played a role in the cultural life of Calcutta. As the founder or co-founder of the first Bengali theatre, his name was not altogether forgotten by Bengali writers, but they have not recognised that Lebediev and his associates represented a new intellectual and social reform movement before the so-called Bengali renaissance under the influence of English education in the 1820s and 30s. Lebediev's writings against the background of that more obscure phase throw a new light on some of the contradictory trends of Bengali national sentiment and westernisation of the next generation, for he was writing about the Bengal of Ram Mohun Roy's early youth.

Neither the full story of Lebediev's adventures and the persecution that he suffered at the hands of the East India Company officials in consequence of his pro-Indian cultural work, nor his remarkable book vindicating Hindu character and custom, appear now to be known in Bengal. Nor is it realised that on return to Russia he made efforts to establish a regular centre for Indian studies and publications, intending to maintain direct contact with Indian men of learning and to exchange with them the best of Indian and Russian literature for mutual benefit. For this purpose he was the first person probably to make a Bengali type font.

His ideas in the field of oriental studies and international cultural intercourse were bold and original. He was bold enough to criticise the great Sir William Jones on the matter of Sanscrit and sane enough to plead for the serious cultivation of despised "vernaculars" and to insist that Hindustani itself was something more than a corrupt "jargon". But above all he stood for welcoming Indians into a free and equal participation in the learned world of Europe.

The scanty European knowledge of Sanscrit and Indology was then monopolised by second rate dilettanti among the English officials who hired or cajoled pundits and munshis to supply them with materials and picked their brains without acknowledgment. Except for Lebediev it was not until Max Muller that any European scholar honestly asserted that Sanscrit could not be studied without the basis of Indian learned tradition and the authority of Indian scholars. It was with a burning sense of wrong, on behalf of his friends and teachers, that Lebediev exposed the literary pretensions as well as the commercial avarice and oppressive rule of the Company "jackals".

When Lebediev had acquired enough of the language he started to translate English plays into Bengali. His friends corrected and improved the translations, transposing the scene and characters to an Indian setting. The first play was an ephemeral English farce of no literary value, but the adaptation of the western social setting and manners to an Indian background was something entirely new and a significant adventure both in ideas and in language. The Bengali colleagues headed by Golak Nath Das enthusiastically set about collecting and training a Bengali caste and Lebediev sank all his money into building a new theatre "decorated after the Bengali style". The first performances were highly successful and promised well for the future.

Meanwhile the manager of an English theatre began an intrigue against Lebediev, foisted on him an English business partner who deliberately entangled him in debt and finally attempted to burn down the theatre. Lebediev found himself beset on every side, flouted by the law courts, his teaching connections ruined and his resources gone. In desperation he wrote to friends and patrons in Russia, begging for a little aid and above all for some protection as a Russian subject against his persecutors. But help was long in arriving, and it was two or three years before Lebediev could find his way back to Russia.

Meanwhile he took refuge probably with Shah Alum II, who, if nothing else, was a great lover of music, and became Theatrical Director at the Court of the Moghul. Of this passage in Lebediev's strange career we know little. Strained relations between England and Russia made it undesirable afterwards to advertise a connection which might have looked as though the Russian government (Lebediev became a minor government official on return to Russia) had its agents in India in the tense period of Anglo–French struggle for supremacy in the East. To add to Lebediev's difficulties, about the time he was leaving India a Russian army was actually under orders to invade India from the North, and it may have been for that reason that Lebediev, temporarily stranded in London in 1801, published his Hindustani grammar with a polite dedication to the Directors of the East India Company. But what he really thought, and what he had really seen in India, he kept for his personal journal and that unfortunately is still unpublished and now lies with five volumes of his M.S. notes and translations in a Moscow library tantalisingly out of reach.

Lebediev not only propagated Bengali cultural nationalism but foretold in quite clear terms a coming struggle for Indian independence. Political freedom, he maintained, was essential if humanity were to benefit fully by India's great achievements in the past and her potential contribution to civilisation in the future. It is not conceivable that he would not have discussed such notions with Indian friends, perhaps adopted their views on the subject. But in any case he was not only the partisan of Indian aspirations then but served his friends by putting on record a clue to the first beginnings of the freedom movement in Bengal.

Lebediev believed that the new knowledge of India in Europe could "create a bond among the human race scattered over the face of the earth". A deeper understanding of religious and moral truth would "spread through the world and strengthen the mutual bonds of friendship desirable among nations and unite their abilities for the establishment of a general and universal well being."

In conclusion it can be said that though the records of Russian travellers to India are scanty, these chance individual accounts are different from those left to us by others. These records are, therefore, of value to us. In the main they are sympathetic and friendly records. Whatever the status or the background of the Russian traveller might be, his outlook was essentially different from that of the French, English or Portuguese travellers, who saw India from the point of view of conquerors or would be exploiters of her wealth.

(*ISCUS—A Journal of the Indo-Soviet Cultural Society*, May 1954)

29

Maxim Gorky and the National Liberation Movement in India

Eve Lyusternik

Important new features appeared in India's struggle for independence at the beginning of this century. It was the first time that stable links were established between the country's national liberation movement and the revolutionary forces in western Europe.

Some revolution-minded Indian patriots gained inspiration from Gorky's fiction and publicistic works. One of these was Bhikaiji Rustom Kama,[1] an Indian revolutionary who gathered around her the more resolute and selfless champions of India's freedom, living in Paris and other Western European cities.

Mikhail Pavlovich (Veltman), an Orientalist and revolutionary, often met Kama and her associates in Paris and wrote about these meetings later in his memoirs entitled Revolutionary Silhouettes: "Kama showed a keen interest in revolutionary events in Russia, especially the revolution of 1905, and in the role of the working class, and was familiar with a number of works of the theory of Marxism. Of the Russian writers Gorky was the one who interested her most of all and once she asked me to tell her the gist of his famous poem about the Falcon.[2] When I did so, she asked me to get the poem for her and translate it into French. I remember there were tears of happiness in her eyes when I finally presented her with a translation, poorly done but beautifully written, of *Song of the Falcon*. 'This poem,' said Kama deeply moved, 'is better than any propaganda staff.' " Kama followed the development of the Russian revolution very closely and before my departure for Russia in August 1917 she gave me a letter for Gorky with a request to publish it in Russia. Regrettably, the letter was lost.

For his part, Gorky was deeply interested in the destiny of India and the liberation struggle of its people. In the autumn of 1912 he proposed that Kama and Krishnawarma, a prominent member of the Indian national liberation movement and editor of *The Indian Sociologist* journal, contribute to the Russian journal *Sovremennik.*

Gorky asked Kama to send an article for the Russian press about "The Indian Woman, Her Current Status and Role in India's Struggle for Freedom". He wrote: "Russian democracy and Russian women will be much obliged to you for telling them about the life and struggle of the people living on the banks of the Ganges, the democrats and the women of great India."

Kama replied immediately, saying that she was devoting all her time and efforts to the cause of her country and its struggle: "... I shall do my very best to comply with your request."

The article that Gorky asked for was not printed in *Sovremennik.* Instead, Gorky included in the "Foreign News" column that he ran, a Russian translation of Kama's article *Indian Siren,* which she had published earlier, and which, according to him, "exposed the English writer Annie Besant, the friend and associate of our theosophist, the late Elena Blavatskaya.[3] The Russian reader will be interested to know about Mme. Besant's[4] evolution."

What was it about Annie Besant that attracted Gorky and what was it that Kama condemned?

Besant, English by birth, was an active member of the Theosophical Society and became its president in 1907. She moved to India in 1893 and linked her whole life and activity with that country. She continued to be the leader of the

Theosophical Society and at the same time became involved in educational activity.

At the turn of the century Besant joined the Indian National Congress and cooperated with the moderate liberal wing. In 1907 after the radical democrats (the so-called "extremists") were ousted from the National Congress, and on the eve of the First World War, Besant tried to reconcile the "extremists" with the "moderates" on the political platform of the drive for self-government within the boundaries of the British Empire. India's political emigrants, the selfless champions of the country's independence, condemned the stand as defeatist, and this was what Kama expressed in her article that aroused Gorky's interest. At the time of acute struggle in Russia between the revolutionary and reactionary forces, Gorky believed it would be very useful to acquaint the Russian reader with the political struggle in India.

Gorky's letter of 20 October 1912 to Krishnawarma has not been preserved in his archives and its contents became known only after the Indian historian, Yadjnik Indilal, published the text in a monograph devoted to the life and activities of Krishnawarma.[5] The letter shows how highly Gorky assessed the Indian people's contribution to the development of the material culture and intellectual life of humanity and the importance he attached to the liberation struggle of the Indians and the establishment of friendly relations between the democratic forces of Russia and India. Gorky wrote: "Thank you very much for sending me *The Indian Sociologist.* I shake your hand, the hand of an indefatigable champion for the freedom of Great India, the freedom of the Indian people who have given mankind instances of profound insight into the spiritual life of man.

"Could I ask you to write an article for the *Russian Review* which would give the Russian democrats an idea of the Indian people's movement for freedom and justice. A historical article would be most desirable with an indication of the facts that give the best illustration of the Indians' struggle for their freedom. The article should consist of 60,000 or 80,000 Ms and, if possible, it should arrive in time for the January issue. The translation will be done by the most competent translator.

"I would greatly appreciate it if you could fulfil my request. We must prove to our peoples that all those who want justice and a life that is in accord with reason should come to understand their unity of purpose and spirit and unite into a single force capable of completely defeating evil on earth.

"You, Krishnawarma, are the Mazzini[6] of India; you know the aspirations of your great nation and you will certainly understand that the Russian people should know about the life of modern India.

"Eagerly awaiting your reply, I wish you much health and happiness.

M. Gorky

Villa Seraphina, Capri,

October 20, 1912[7]"

In his reply dated 28 October 1912, Krishnawarma thanked Gorky but turned down the offer to write an article for the Russian magazine saying he had no time for literary work. He enclosed clippings from *The Indian Sociologist* and suggested that Gorky write the article himself using the material he was sending him and making references to Krishnawarma because the materials reflected his views.

Gorky used the clippings to write an article about India which appeared in the "Foreign News" column in the eleventh issue of *Sovremennik*. "Look how fast the Indian national liberation movement and its struggle against British domination is growing. *The Indian Sociologist*, a publication put out in Paris by the nationalist Krishnawarma, whom the Indians are fond of comparing with Mazzini and for whom they predict the same future as Garibaldi's,[8] gives a very accurate picture of the relations between the Indians and the English."

The grounds for such assumptions were the changes that took place in Krishnawarma's political views in connection with the upsurge of the national liberation movement in India in 1905–08 influenced by the revolution in Russia.

Living in emigration in London, he sided with the moderate liberal trend in the Indian National Congress which, guided by Italy's experience, was emulating Mazzini, while Garibaldi was the model political leader for the radical democratic wing of the Indian national liberation movement. Persecuted by the British authorities, Krishnawarma left London in 1907 and settled in Paris where he came into close contact with emigre Indian revolutionaries. That same year he founded, together with Kama, a group of Indian emigrants and became their leader. His activities took on certain new aspects. Formerly a supporter of passive methods of resistance, he began to call for a general strike, believing that strikes were "the modern weapon of revolution".

However, the hope of seeing Krishnawarma as an Indian Garibaldi did not materialise; he remained a moderate liberal though he continued his tireless drive against British oppression in India.[9]

The twelfth issue of *Sovremennik* carried Krishnawarma's letter to William Taft, the then President of the United States. The document is of much interest today.

Gorky prefaced the letter with a short elucidation of the document and acquainted the reader with its author.

What prompted Krishnawarma's open letter to Taft was the President's address to the American envoy in London on the occasion of the 300th anniversary of the translation of the Bible. Taft made use of the occasion to declare the US ruling class's disinterested striving to ensure universal peace among nations and for that purpose he proposed creating a union between the USA, Great Britain and the other Western powers. His aim was to consolidate the reactionary forces of both hemispheres in the interest of the bourgeoisie, particularly the American bourgeoisie, to struggle against revolutionary and national-liberation movements. The peace-making speeches were intended to give the USA the reputation of the champion of peace among nations.

President Taft has gone down in history as a zealous defender of the "big stick" policy and "dollar diplomacy". It was he who strangled the insurrection in Cuba in 1906, who inspired the intervention in Nicaragua in 1912 and who choked the strike movement in the United States.

In his letter to the President, Krishnawarma revealed the deep-rooted contradictions between the declaration of universal peace and the methods suggested for its establishment by the usurpers of freedom and independence of nations. The Indian patriot wrote that Taft's proposals "would sooner create even greater hostility and bloodshed rather than eliminate them."

Krishnawarma's explanation for the British government's readiness to ally itself with the USA on the terms proposed by Taft was that the alliance would give Britain the possibility "to continue its policy of plunder and oppression of the countries to which it had brought destruction and annihilation."

Krishnawarma found Taft's allusion to Britain as the Mother Country amusing and even comical. He detected falsehood in the President's address and a threat to the liberation movement in his country: "In conclusion I shall take the liberty of telling you, dear Sir, that until all the enslaved peoples of the world are free or until the countries which yearn for peace do not take up the cause with clean hands, we, the representatives of the enslaved nations, will never stop for a single moment disrupting the universal peace with our struggle for liberation from political slavery."[10]

Gorky also included in the "Foreign News" column a letter of congratulation from Krishnawarma to Sun Yat-sen, "a most energetic champion for his country's freedom", on the occasion of the establishment of the Chinese republic.

Notes

1. Bhikaiji Rustom Kama (née Petit, 1875—?), Indian" journalist and public figure. Devoted her whole life to the struggle for the liberation of India. She was interested in the Russian revolutionary movement and had contacts with Russian political emigrants in Paris.
2. *Song of the Falcon* by Gorky.

3. Elena Blavatskaya (1831–1891), Russian writer who founded the Theosophical Society (together with Colonel G. Alcott) in New York in 1875.
4. *Sovremennik*, 1912, No 10, p. 379.
5. Yagnik Indulal, Shyamaji Krishnawarma (*Life and Times of an Indian Revolutionary*), Bombay, 1950, pp. 305–306.
6. Giuseppe Mazzini (1805–1872), an active participant in the 1848–49 Revolution and head of the government of the Roman Republic.
7. Eve Lyusternik, *Russian-Indian Economic, Scientific and Cultural Relations in the 19th Century*, Moscow, Nauka Publishers, 1966, p. 198.
8. *Sovremennik*, 1912, No 11, p. 392.
9. Towards the end of his life Krishnawarma retired from political activity and settled down in Geneva where he lived in complete seclusion. Jawaharlal Nehru, who visited him in 1926, later recalled that "his pockets were crammed full of old copies of *The Indian Sociologist* which he used to publish. He had a habit of taking them out and indicating excitedly some article or another that he had written decades ago (...) He always spoke of the past (...), of various persons whom the British government had sent to spy on him, of how he guessed who they were and could easily twist them round his little finger (...). He was a relic of the past and had clearly outlived his time (...). Yet there was something of the old fire in his eyes, and though there was little in common between us, I could not but feel a certain sympathy and respect for him."
10. *Sovremennik*, 1912, No 12, pp. 408–411.

(*Soviet Literature*, 1989)